AMERICA'S COLORFUL RAILROADS

Central Vermont's Palmerton Branch local heads through the village of Uncasville, Ct., on Thanksgiving Day 1952. (LIBBY)

AMERICA'S COLORFUL RAILROADS

Don Ball, Jr.

BONANZA BOOKS
New York

TO LINDA

Without Whose Help

"PATIENCE" AND "UNDERSTANDING" might best describe the durable qualities of the contributors to this book. "Friends" would be another word. For years I have been trying to get this book into print, and for *years* I have been sitting on the original slides that have been reproduced in this volume. Many, many times I have said, "Hold on a little longer," and they have. Their reward, I hope, is now in this finished product, as no words of mine can adequately express my sincere and deep appreciation for their faith in me and the project.

I have mentioned Tom Donahue and John Pickett as "active rooters," and certainly Chic Kerrigan saw to it that I "kept the faith," even after three false starts. Bob Collins, who has helped me with every book, has once again been more than generous. I am indebted to Bob on many counts—we all are, for look at how many authors Bob has helped with so much of his fine photography! Tom Harley and I broke an endurance record, going through 800 slides at a clip, looking for *just the right one;* Roger Plummer and I did similarly, coming up with some southwest gems that otherwise wouldn't be in the book. Henry Libby, Steve Bogen, Gary Widell, Bridget Cavanaugh, Jim LaVake, Dick Wallin, Allan Vaughn and Eugene Van Dusen all came forth with just what I was looking for.

Don Ackland, my Publisher, more than anyone outside the sphere of rail-friendships, believed in the project and helped me keep my faith in it alive. I appreciate the genuine personal friendship that has developed out of our healthy quarrels. Bernie Schleifer once again made masterful work out of my demands for picture content and cropping. There should be more Bernie Schleifers in this world—we'd all get along better! Gypsy da Silva has been a pearl, seeing to it that I leave out most of the bangs (my beloved exclamation points) that would otherwise be included!!! and tying up myriad of editorial details. She developed a great personal interest in this book and expressed it by going the extra mile. Editorial content was left intact.

Much credit is due Bill Schaumburg for his fine maps and to Jim Boyd for making my life easier with his eloquent Epilogue on the technical side and "next generation" side of the railfan hobby. I only wish I hadn't turned my back on the 9912A when I encountered her while chasing Burlington steam fantrips! And while I'm at it, much appreciation goes to Hal Carstens of Carstens Publications who not only gave advice to my publisher on the magazine side of the rail hobby but also "turned his back" once or twice, enabling Bill and Jim to finish their contributions in the face of deadlines!

My wife, Linda, has supported this project through thick and thin, and likewise my kids. I love 'em all dearly.

Finally—a word of thanks to my Mom. Many are the times she let me go off to distant rail yards. She trusted me at the bicycle-riding age, and because of her love and support, I grew with the hobby. These were rich years indeed.

This edition is published by Bonanza Books, a division of Crown Publishers, Inc., by arrangement with Reed Books/ Addison House, Inc., Danbury, N.H.
        d e f g h

BONANZA 1980 EDITION
Manufactured in the United States of America
Designed by Bernard Schleifer

CONTENTS

COLOR WAS FOR FUN   vi

THE PHOTOGRAPHERS   8

1. UP NORTH, DOWN EAST   1

2. GOTHAM AND BEYOND   41

3. FROM DIXIE TO THE MIDLANDS   81

4. MAIN LINES OF MID-AMERICA   121

5. DISTANT HORIZONS   161

EPILOGUE by Jim Boyd   201

COLOR WAS FOR FUN

THIS BOOK BEGAN on a rainy spring weekend, many years ago. For a long time, I had been promising my Mom I would clean my stuff (as she put it) out of her attic but managed to avoid the chore as long as I possibly could. Now that my Dad had passed on, Mom was getting ready to put the house on the market and look for an apartment. The time had definitely come, and I committed myself well in advance to a Saturday—all day. I marked the date on my calendar. The days of promises, promises—empty rhetoric—on the matter would soon be over.

That Saturday dawned red, then gray, and then rain; perfect weather, I suppose, for working inside. There would be no real surprises in store for I have always been a great collector of things and was ready for anything. After my first couple of hours in the attic, I was convinced I had saved *everything* and had spared nothing. My whole life seemed to be filed (piled) away in boxes! Timetables from the very first day I started bothering ticket agents for them, sketches made in 8th grade General Science class, notes to and from high school girl friends, maps, a flashlight from camp, post cards, my Boy Scout knife, 78 rpm records, playbills, letters, yearbooks, ticket stubs, hats from dances, pictures by the *thousands* . . . why I even had my very first toys saved. And stashed away in a box were a hundred or so Missouri state sales tokens earmarked for the railroad tracks (the lead in 'em to be flattened out larger than pennies). I found a life of long lost treasures and wonderful memories in boxes—a lifetime I could not go through in one day.

Sometime during that *first* day in Mom's attic, I was reminded of Tevye's song in *Fiddler on the Roof* about tradition and its message that life offers its possession of old customs from generation to generation. In the play, the significance of having one's intangible possessions was that it made life enjoyable, as was the case with his fellow villagers who were harshly treated and kicked around, never being able to settle down. Tevye sings: "Because of tradition, everyone of us knows who he is and what God expects him to be . . . Without tradition, our life is as shakey as a fiddler on the roof." I guess I had gone one step further: keeping all my traditions and my quite tangible possessions.

I felt a shiver go through me as I opened a very large carton filled to the gunwales with old gray steel slide file boxes. I had always taken slides of scenery, buildings (particularly barns and 18th-century clapboard structures), family, girl friends, cars, parties—generally subjects I loved, but knew I would rarely require prints of. (With trains, of course, a negative was required to make the desired enlargements.) I found my first slides labeled "Christmas, 1951–Spring, 1952" and promptly began the treasure hunt, using a plastic hand viewer I had stashed away. Robbie in her new dress . . . I'd forgotten her. Mom and Dad, my sister, grandmother. The house almost covered with snow, my friends sledding down the hill, our car . . . Lo and behold, a steam locomotive! Everything was filed chronologically, regardless of subject, and here was my very first slide taken of a train (or rather, an engine, in this case). It struck me as quite amusing that this first 35 mm slide was taken of Jersey Central's doughty old 0-6-0 #101 switching some heavyweight head end cars in Jersey City! This diminutive U.S.R.A. switcher was as homey a creature, and as unlikely a subject—and railroad—as I could imagine. #101 had apparently even lost her number plate somewhere along the way and now was just wearing a steel plate bearing the carefully stenciled numerals "101." She must have been slow of speech and soft in tongue, but nevertheless, she had commanded the attention of my new camera. Saturday became Sunday.

Barbara; the '34 Ford Phaeton; country drives; an air show with B-36s and F-84s; the New Haven . . . ; beach parties; then Fall—a pumpkin patch and more barns. Central Vermont, Boston & Maine, football, and another Christmas. Spring, lovely Spring, and treasure-of-treasures, the summer trains of Lawrence! Rock Island's crimson and maroon diesels, UP's 4-12-2s, Santa Fe . . . Into '54 and '55—more goodies at trackside, Marcia, my folks' '51 Olds convertible with eight people in it! The new '55 Ford. '56 and '57 were not such good years; I had forsaken Kodachrome for the slightly faster Anscochrome. Here were Burlington 0-5s I had paced westward out of Omaha toward Lincoln, now green; and here were IC 4-8-2s and L&N 2-8-4s now sporting green. Back to Kodachrome. Bless Kodachrome. Indiana's farewell fun . . . corn fields, fraternity parties, a harvest moon, Carol on a wall, a grab shot on the Monon, every angle of DePauw, an ROTC trip, a weekend in Chicago, graduation . . . More years, more boxes, no more time. It was obvious I had taken much more color than I remembered. My black-and-white negatives I knew. But the color . . .

The closest I ever came to taking slides seriously was when, while in college, I sold duplicates made from several favorite orginals through an ad in *Railroad* magazine—purely as a diversion from pledge duties. What little income there was went as a contribution to the pizza fund.

I took the bull by the horns and the boxes of slides and carefully placed them in the trunk of the car to take home. I pulled every train slide out of the thousands of slides that resided in those boxes. I did not get much else accomplished in the attic that weekend, but I did come up with a surprisingly good number of train slides I had taken over the years. I bought new plastic file boxes and filed what I had by railroad and in chronological order.

The idea for a color book really jelled when I became interested in railfanning again with diesels. Slide shows were the vogue, and 8 x 10s and 11 x 14s were no longer desired for trading. A generation had passed. Tom Donahue and John Pickett, whose black-and-white work has appeared in all of my books, enthusiastically "nudged" me on the idea of doing a big railroad color book, and Chic Kerrigan, more than anyone, downright *pushed* (in the literary sense of the word)! I am grateful that he did.

Now, a word about 35 mm slide cameras and color photography. I have always abhored carrying a lot of cameras around, looking like a "goop." I don't like anything around my neck and have an even greater distaste for big bulky camera bags. I could never walk around being a professional photographer. The 35 mm camera, on the other hand, is just right for the spur-of-the-moment (grab) shots and can be carried unobtrusively in one hand—carefully! Without it, I would have been lost on many an occasion. I guess I look at the camera as simply an extension of me—a mechanical extension, if you will, to document a moment I want to preserve. And nothing can be as heartbreaking as a lost moment that was all-at-once intensively enjoyed but now gone forever. Here's where that 35 can be a pal. With steam railroading, I gladly lugged the 4 x 5 Graflex D around, film packs and all, but that too was shelved in favor of a smaller model T Rollei and later a Hasselblad. The 35 mm, for me, has finally come into its own.

And what about the other rail photographers? What did they use in these pioneering days of color rail photography? Tom Harley led off with a pre-war Kodak 35 with an f3.5 lens with a shutter speed of 1/200 sec. (Tom's first efforts include the two fine shots he took of the Santa Fe in Chicago in 1941 that appear in this book.) Chic Kerrigan started color in 1946, using a Kodak Bantam Special sporting an f.2 Ektar 45 mm lens with a shutter speed of 1/400 sec. (His first exposure is the Milwaukee 4-8-4 at West Lake Forest, in this book. Nice work!) This camera used 828 film with a grand total of eight exposures to a roll of film. Tom Donahue inaugurated his Kodak 35 Rangefinder in 1941 just before Uncle Sam found other things for Tom to do. The camera had an f3.5 lens and shutter speed of 1/200 sec. In 1945, Tom went all out and bought a Leica with an f.2 Summar lens and a snappy 1/500 sec. shutter speed—about the best one could get to handle an ASA of 10. John Pickett broke in his new Prak-tiflex single lens reflex on the Rutland in late 1950, changing over to a Zeiss Contaflex in 1955. "Van" Van Dusen, a pioneer black and white photographer from the early '30s, was more the norm, starting into his world of color with an Argus C-3 in November of '47 and eventually work-ing up to a Leica. Today most of the contributors have gone to the Japanese SLRs with the system approach. As for myself, I started 35 mm color at the end of 1951 with a Kodak Pony 135 with a 51 mm Anaston lens, an aperture of f4.5 and a top shutter speed of 1/200 sec. The lens was surprisingly sharp under ideal conditions (a standing train under sunny skies), and soon I moved up to everyone's camera, the beloved brick: an Argus C-3 with a 50 mm Cintar f3.5 lens and a slightly higher shutter speed of 1/300 sec. In 1957, the sturdy old Argus was side-tracked for a secondhand Retina 1 with a 50 mm Schneider Xenar f2.8 lens and a whopping shutter speed of 1/500 sec. At last—the fastest train could be stopped.

Finally, railroad color was not a radical departure from the norm with that 1951 Christmas camera. In 1946, and '47, I pushed many a roll of Kodacolor through my Eastman Kodak Brownie Reflex and mostly diesel at that. I still have the little 1"-square 127 orange negatives that to this day can produce an 8"-square enlargement of the Santa Fe's *Kansas Cityan* passing the foot of our street; I still have the gleaming CGW in Kan-sas City, and the 2-10-2s and 4-12-2s of Lawrence. Wabash E-7s on the *City of St. Louis* running on the Union Pacific, and Rock Island's 5000s, 5100s, and my favorite-of-favorites *Rocket* paint schemes. I know that diesels had a subtle hand at this; Missouri Pacific's beautiful timetable diesels *had* to be taken in color, and Rock Island's E-6 that appeared in General Motors ads deserved nothing short of Kodacolor. Some of those new fancy train ads were nothing short of new visions of blinding loveli-ness, and I *had* to duplicate them in color!

I have saved most of my cameras, and one of these days I fully intend to resurrect the predecessor of my Brownie Reflex, my beloved Brownie box camera. Eastman Kodak Company's slogan for the box camera went, "You press the button, we do the rest." I fully intend to put the camera—and Kodak—to the test!

1

UP NORTH, DOWN EAST

BANGOR AND AROOSTOOK RAILROAD CO.
BOSTON AND MAINE RAILROAD
CANADIAN NATIONAL RAILWAYS
CANADIAN PACIFIC RAILWAY
CENTRAL VERMONT RAILWAY, INC.
DELAWARE AND HUDSON RAILROAD CORPORATION
DELAWARE, LACKAWANNA AND WESTERN RAILROAD CO.
ERIE RAILROAD
LEHIGH AND HUDSON RIVER RAILWAY CO.
LEHIGH AND NEW ENGLAND RAILROAD CO.
LONG ISLAND RAIL ROAD CO.
MAINE CENTRAL RAILROAD CO.
NEW YORK CENTRAL SYSTEM
NEW YORK, NEW HAVEN AND HARTFORD RAILROAD CO.
PENNSYLVANIA RAILROAD
RUTLAND RAILWAY CORP.

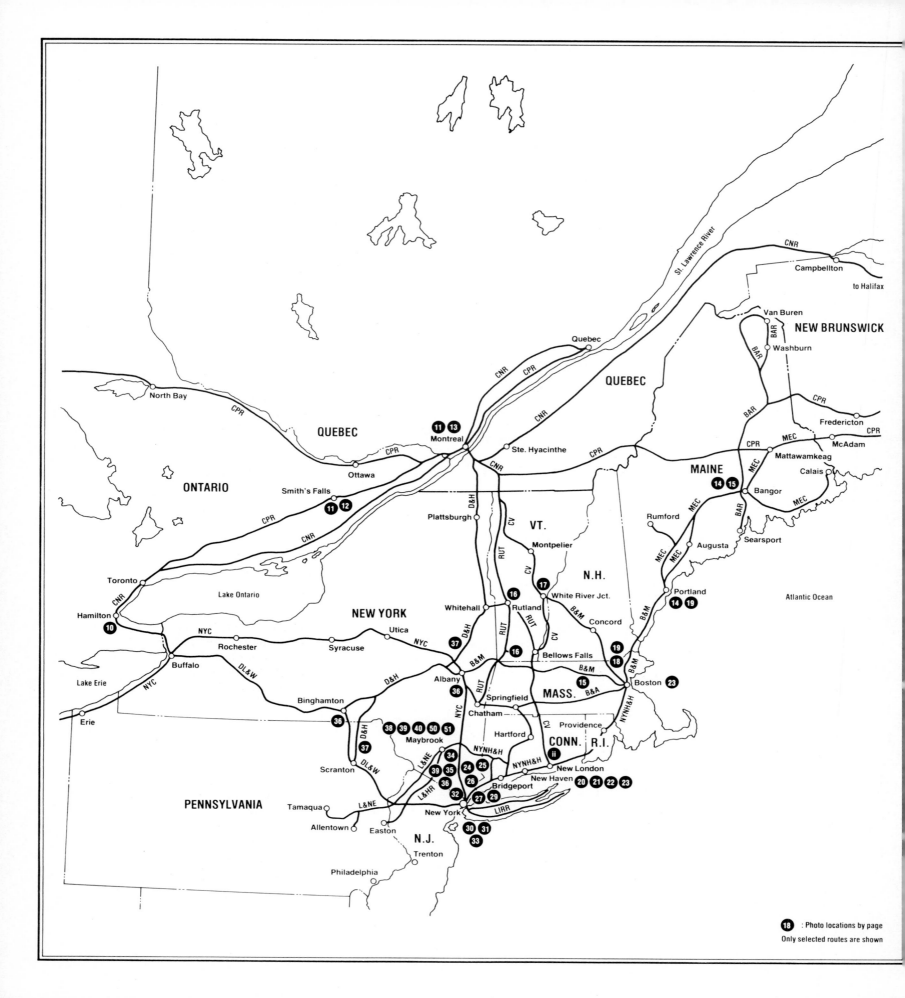

: Photo locations by page

Only selected routes are shown

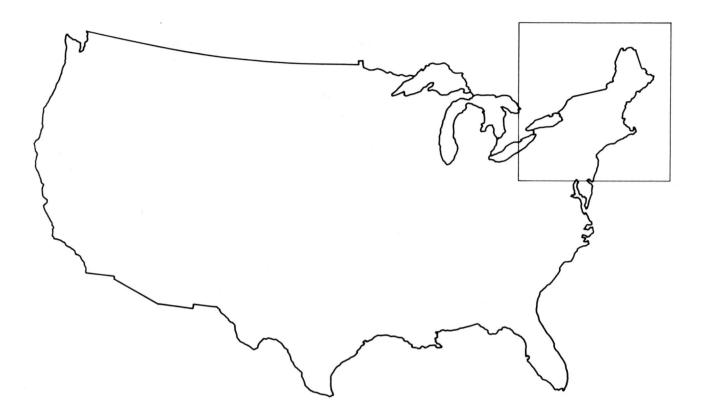

10	Bayview, Ont.
14	Rigby, Me.
14-15	No. Maine Jct.
15	Worcester, Mass.
16	Bennington, Vt.
18	Deerfield, Mass.
18	Winchester, Mass.
19	Wakefield, Mass.
20, 22	Leetes Island, Ct.
21	Old Saybrook, Ct.
21	Branford, Ct.
23	East Haven, Ct.
24	Uncasville, Ct.
25	Beacon Falls, Ct.
26	New Rochelle, N.Y.
27	Devon, Ct.
29	Greens Farms, Ct.
30	Long Island City (Sunnyside), N.Y.
31	Jamaica, L.I.
32	Spuyten Duyvil (Bronx), N.Y.
33	Mott Haven (Bronx), N.Y.
34-5	Harmon, N.Y.
36	Rensselaer, N.Y.
37	Saratoga Springs, N.Y.
37	Carbondale, Pa.
39	Warwick, N.Y.

MY FONDEST MEMORY under catenary took place three days into spring on a dreary March 24th afternoon in 1955. I had heard of a new passenger electric locomotive on the New Haven. I knew it was a new ignitron rectifier locomotive from GE, "similar in design" to a pair of experimental rectifier locomotives in use on the Pennsylvania. I had also heard of a supposed race between one of these new electrics and a Pennsy GG-1, each trailing eighteen P-70 coaches. As the story went, the New Haven job was pulling ahead of the G when, at 105 miles an hour, the GE man in the cab ordered "shut it down!" We heard of tests on Hell Gate with incredible loads, with the passenger-geared engine pulling amps to the point that the pantograph-to-trolley contact (shoe) wasn't a sufficient conductor for the current being drawn by the traction motors. Employees joked about the gang foreman of the wire train obtaining clearances to work on "any and all" circuits that might be de-energized on Hell Gate after each test! The first revenue passenger run of the new EP-5 was *not* to receive advance press. (That would be done at a later public unveiling.) I got a call the night before No. 370 was to make the first revenue runs on the westbound *Colonial* and eastbound *Senator*. Hell Gate Bridge seemed the choice spot for photography; using it entailed getting a release for the long walk out on the approach spans to the bridge itself. Once I was out on the bridge, one of New Haven's distinctive Hunter green and yellow EF-3 freight motors sounded her air horn and rumbled past with westbound symbol HG-3 to Bay Ridge, both of her pantographs up. A few minutes after HG-3's caboose was out of sight, another Hunter green and yellow motor, this time a "flat-bottom," rumbled through the span with the EB *Colonial*. At precisely 4:12 P.M., No. 370 hummed into sight, dazzling in the new McGuines red, black and white dress. A bombshell in paint! At once, I fell in love with this arresting, powerpacked machine. Over the years, I've gotten to ride, and know, each of the ten "jets"—they couldn't be called anything else! The fastest one, the one with the 7-mph discrepancy on her speedometer, the electrical "trouble maker," etc., and I have a fond affection for all of them.

Over on the New York Central, there seemed to be far less personality to their various motors than on the New Haven. Sure, the Central had the fleet of the famed "Ives tinplate" class-S motors dating back to 1904, and they had the thirty-six work horse T-motors riding on B-B+B-B span bolster trucks and using the identical basic gearless design that the original S-class motors used, but somehow, the engines were of the same mold—one of representing little power or importance in their visual appearance. Antiquated. Across the land, as American locomotive building progressed, scale and power—and looks—expanded and changed to a degree that rapidly rendered all previous forms of motive power archaic. Not so with Central's electrics. Personal opinion. In the mid-fifties, the T-class and P-class motors (the latter being the largest-on-the-Central ex-Cleveland Union Terminal electrics) received the same dashing lightning stripe paint jobs the road diesels had, and the resulting "change" was nothing short of magnificent! I commuted into and out of New York behind these engines for several years, and the stripes conveyed a classic individuality to Central's electrics. Less than a decade later, I would become a New Haven commuter and the old allegiance I felt toward the New Haven would grow even stronger.

I have made countless trips head-end in the diesels and electrics of the New Haven, and I shall never be fully resigned to the passing of the various New Haven electrics. For me, certainly for any operating employee, as well as for those knowledgeable about the New Haven's electric operations, there will always be bitter regret over the complete phasing out of these great machines. Why, not really so long ago, I was relaxing in the last car of the 5:52 out of Grand Central. It had been a tiring day and one thing was on my mind—sleep! We pulled out of Grand Central, and in a while I was lulled to sleep over the rail joints, ticket in plain sight in shirt pocket for the conductor. Shortly, I was awakened by what seemed to be abnormally rough track. Fellow commuters momentarily forgot their evening papers, turned to the windows and to each other. On the first sharp curve, I could see that we had a "jet" (EP-5 rectifier) on the head end. We were now braking where the diesels usually are still accelerating—through Pelham Manor, approaching New Rochelle Jct. I knew I could go back to sleep. I also knew I'd be home on time! Quite often, to this day, a conductor friend will quip about wishing we had a "jet"—or "flat-bottom"—this morning, or a "tiger," or whatever, referring to the long-gone electrics. He'll grumble about late schedules and the diesel's loss of time between stations. I'll glance out the window at the fascinating pattern of triangular catenary and remember better days. Progress. . . .

From my point of view, electric railroading was (is) always an interesting subject to follow. For like steam, the main line electric railroad operations in the United States were all different; each operation was unique to the particular railroad in its method of generation, transmission, collection and application of motive power. Going back into railroad history, several railroads turned toward electrification at the turn of the century in hopes of finding a better and more efficient motive power than steam. During the first two decades of the century, great advances were made in the general development of electric locomotives; the invention of multiple-unit control; direct-current regeneration; high speed circuit breakers; automatic substation and refinement of 60-cycle converters and motor generators. Other contributions to the art included the first successful high-voltage alternating current system; notably the Westinghouse 11,000 volt, 25-cycle, single-phase (AC) system for the New Haven in June of 1907, and the design of the high speed gearless passenger locomotive, notably New York Central's S-class locomotive in 1904 (some of which still work in Grand Central Terminal!) and Milwaukee's bipolar motors in 1918.

Almost immediately, the railroads that chose to electrify found that electric locomotive designs offered relatively unlimited capacity as far as tractive effort and speed were concerned. Furthermore, it was quickly determined that the service availability of electric locomotives approached an incredible 95 percent. With the centralization of power generation and the development of efficient long distance power transmission, the railroads had instant pulling power when and where needed, with the ability to shut it off without incurring "idle-time" (stand by) losses. The initial costs of electrification discouraged (as it does today) many a railroad from going into it, even though substantially improved train operation at proportionally lower maintenance costs was assured where there was heavy density traffic. With few exceptions, therefore, electrification of steam railroads in the United States was limited to high-density traffic corridors, along with certain terminal areas around large cities.

In the 1930s the diesel-electric locomotive emerged on the railroad scene. Up until then, all motive power competition and comparison was strictly between steam and electric. During the succeeding three decades, engineers representing various interests went on to assemble data on all three types of motive power and where each type was most efficient. I *still* question some of their findings.

In the '30s and '40s, when the streamlining fad hit the railroads, the designers turning to electric locomotives no longer were dealing with the power source. They had to get along without the sense of vitality that power sources seem to transmit visually. The energy-to-rail electric power came from small motors hidden between small, or medium-size driving wheels, with all of the accompanying electrical gear covered by a shell. Most electric locomotives possessed nothing more than utilitarian integrity as a result of their not having much to dress up. Herewith lies the rationale that electric locomotives are about as exciting as sewing machine motors. Not so! Back to, or on, the New Haven again; I think back on the thrill I got one morning, late in the era of standard N.H. electrification, when I opened the upper vestibule door and watched our big streamlined double-cab EP-4 (The crews called them "yellow jackets") on the point. She bore down the rails and towered over our long heavy train. Her pantograph reached for those lifeline wires, and effortlessly, those big wheels rolled behind her massive steel frames. Everything was business. Like GG-1, she wore a dress, but behaved like a titan. Child's play! To New Haven, and certainly to many, she (and her freight-hauling look-alikes) was *the embodiment* of the efficient, powerful, swift main line electric locomotive.

Finally, no area in the United States can really be credited for the development of railroads more than New England. That's right, New England. Her sons not only built and ran her own intricate railway systems—practically never calling on outsiders for aid—but also promoted a number of the great roads of the middle and far west, including the first three great transcontinental lines, financing them for the most part, and as Presidents, superintendents, general managers and directors, operating them for many years. And contrary to general belief, American's first railroad was a native New Englander—the Granite Railway, chartered on April 3, 1826, between Milton and Quincy, Mass.

The story of New England itself, and its major railroads has been one of quaintness and individualism, and Yankee inventiveness and ingenuity—qualities often overlooked when it came to recording New England railroading. After all, the first sleeping car was designed by a Massachusetts man, thirty-five years before Pullman, and the first vestibuled train operated through Connecticut in 1857. And did we forget that the ambitious Hoosac Tunnel project through the Berkshires in 1855 was America's first tunneling project? New England's rails gave birth to the pioneer diesel-powered streamliner, *Flying Yankee,* back in 1935, and it was in New England (on the Boston & Maine) where diesel freighters were pioneered—and then operated—in sufficient numbers to lead the region to complete dieselization. New England was a delightful contrast of railroad anachronisms from ponderous 2-10-4 Texas types on the Central Vermont, to diminutive 2-6-0 Moguls that held main assignments on the B&M clear up through dieselization. Bangor & Aroostook, which had the capital to buy the biggest and best, made do with what it had—old engines; their postwar touch of modernity being the diesel powered *Aroostook Flyer* and *Potatoland Special.* Like BAR, the Maine Central managed to operate with 1924 and older vintage steam power until dieselization. During steam's reign, Rutland had the oldest power, excluding four 4-8-2s built in 1946. New Haven of course, had a little of everything—from historic eccentrics and heavy electrics to modern 80"-drivered 4-6-4s—and diesels for every occasion.

Those of us seeking steam in its twilight were almost obliged to skip New England and hunt elsewhere. Those satisfied with B&M's steam commuter trains had a chance. The few who went after New England's colorful array of main line steam power were the photographers who stood at trackside early in the game. We are the richer for their efforts.

In closing this chapter, I want to call attention to the Canadian Pacific and Canadian National. A whole picture book should be done, in color, on Canadian railroads. I have attempted to show some of the arresting main line activity during steam's twilight years in Canada, without showing the charm and particular intricacies of either CPR or CNR. When you consider the fact that CPR often ran Hudsons and Pacifics on freight, ten wheelers on varnish, and 4-4-0s on mixed runs up until the end, then, brother, you've got a lot to show and talk about!

A word on Canada. I've always found Canadian history fascinating as only a small part of it is written down. Canada, like the U.S., is a vast country that was settled at about the same time as the States, but we will never know for sure who was the first European white man who decided to stay. Likewise we will never know who gave the country the name Canada, nor where the word came from! To a railfan, Canada is two giant transcontinental railroads that were forged westward, but once again, recorded history is sketchy. We do know that the Canadian Pacific was chartered by an act of Parliament on February 15, 1881, and completed with a golden spike ceremony at Craigellachie, B.C., on November 7, 1885. Records do indicate a maximum of 24,000 white people were residing in British Columbia at the time, with Winnipeg boasting 7,985 of these inhabitants. But Calgary was not on the map, and across the vast plains, little is documented other than the forts of the fur traders and the tepees of wandering Indians. In striking contrast, when the first transcontinental railroad was completed in the U.S. in 1869, nearly three-quarters of a million people were in the Pacific coast states and well over six million in the states and territories between the Mississippi and the mountains. The progress of U.S. railroad empires and developing west is well documented.

The Canadians that are pictured in this chapter are all "east-enders," where, throughout the fifties, steam was heavily concentrated around the more populated eastern Provinces. Those of us who went north across the border to acquaint ourselves with Canadian steam rediscovered our boyhood past—where youngsters still divided their time between playing baseball and watching trains. And where small town railway stations (we called 'em depots) were still gathering places for folks to jawbone and watch the trains. We relished the fact that Canada was still a place where engineers waved back from their lofty cabs at kids on bikes (or admonished with the whistle the kids hiding behind the freight station, waiting for the engine to flatten their bottle caps and pennies!). Those of us who went north across the border also discovered a little "unwritten history" about the country itself—that the Canadian, like the American, hears in the locomotive whistle the frontier music of his forefathers and the shout of a growing nation.

THE PHOTOGRAPHERS

PHOTOGRAPHER'S CREDITS are listed at the end of each caption in the following sequence: left-hand page, top to bottom; right-hand page, top to bottom. Where all photographs on a page or spread are by the same person, only one name appears.

T. J. DONAHUE

E. T. HARLEY

CHARLES H. KERRIGAN

HENRY S. LIBBY

STEPHEN D. BOGEN

JOHN PICKETT

ROBERT F. COLLINS

MARY ANN CAVANAUGH

GARY WIDELL

JAMES G. LA VAKE

EUGENE VAN DUSEN

ALLAN V. VAUGHN

R. R. WALLIN

JIM BOYD

ROGER S. PLUMMER

I have made it a practice always to open a book with a page or two from Canada; this book will not be an exception. At right, showing the TLC so typically Canadian, Canadian National's 69″-drivered J-4-f class Pacific #5151 has a good roll on merchandise through Fletcher, N. S., en route to Halifax on June 28, 1957. Below, taken on the previous day, two almost spotless Fairbanks Morse CPA-16-5 passenger C-Liners head train No. 59, *The Scotian*, through Dorchester, N. B., on the 840-mile run from Halifax, N. S., to Montreal. Like the cleanliness of the trains, the deep blue sky and tidy surroundings are very much Canadian! (BALL)

Clean, colorful Canadian Camelots! The history of the Canadian railroads closely parallels that of the railroads in the U.S. with the westward transcontinental expansion and the country's subsequent settlements and development. The big difference, of course, is the fact that there are only two major railroads in Canada—the Canadian Pacific and Canadian National. Many of us discovered Canadian steam late in the steam years, but we all delighted in what we saw. The two great Canadian railroads offered a beautiful compromise between the generally massive U.S. engines and the ultra-clean English designs. That green with gold trim, semi-streamlined class U-1-f 4-8-2, at upper left, heading CNR's train No. 5 through the Bayview, Ont., interlocking on Aug. 4, 1958, is a classic example. And, at upper right, CNR's U-2-g class Northern riding the table at Turcot yard, Montreal, on Sept. 3, 1956, sure bulks big for a Canadian . . . but watch out! Seeing can be deceiving. She's light for a 4-8-4 by U.S. standards, but she's a go *anywhere* type of engine—perfect for Canadian rails. My favorite Canadian is at lower right—CPR's striking H-1b class standard Hudson. Built in 1930 by the Montreal Locomotive Works, # 2811 (shown riding the Smiths Falls, Ont., table on Easter Sunday, 1960) is typical of the refined steam power the Canadian Pacific relied on, in contrast to CNR's 4-8-2s and 4-8-4s. I think that this 75″-drivered machine is the quintessence of grace and power—perfectly balanced from pilot to vestibule cab. At lower left, and included just for fun, Canadian National's "Doodlebug" approaches Bayview, en route to Toronto on its "makes-all-stops" schedule. It is shown on June 14, 1958. (BALL, COLLECTION, BALL, DONAHUE)

No other Canadian city has greater variety—color—than Montreal, when it comes to railroading. The Canadian Pacific and Canadian National dominate, of course, but locomotives and equipment from the Boston & Maine, Rutland, Central Vermont, New York Central and Delaware & Hudson frequent the terminus. Both the CPR and CNR call Montreal home and have their head offices in town. Trains of the Canadian Pacific, New York Central, Delaware & Hudson and Boston & Maine use Windsor Station, and the picture, at lower right, is typical of the regular activity at Windsor. In this scene, E-8 # 1800, one of only three E units belonging to CPR, heads the southbound *Alouette* out of the stub end platforms en route to Boston; Pacific # 2527 heads into Windsor with a spic and span commuter run. In the background, a New York Central RS-3 is on the point of the arriving *Montreal Limited*. At upper right, G3g # 2394 is fresh from an overhaul at the Angus shops and is shown ready to depart for Veudreuil on July 2, 1956. Above, in April 1960, Canadian Pacific's 4-6-4 # 2811 is framed in a perfect ¾ wedge shot, eating up the 128 miles between Montreal and Smiths Falls, Que., over the Winchester Subdivision with a passenger extra. That warm red wine color . . . was anything prettier? (DONAHUE, BALL, BALL)

New England's railroads were certainly colorful in their own right, from history and lore, to motive power and trains. New England's two northern roads are the Maine Central and Bangor & Aroostook, each having connections at the Canadian border. The Maine Central is pictured above, and at upper right, with a trusty 1913 vintage 2-8-0 getting out of Rigby, Me., in September 1949, and a pair of modern EMD F-3s at Worcester, Mass., on the B&M in September 1952. Although the Maine Central is an independent line, it works very closely with financial partner Boston & Maine, MeC's principal traffic source. This close relationship accounts for the Maine Central units on the B&M (and vice versa) and the almost identical paint schemes on both roads' Fs and E-7s. One has to look very closely at one of the on-coming maroon and gold units to see if it has the "Pine Tree" herald or the "Minute Man" herald.

Kennebeck, Irish Cobbler, Katahdin, Green Mountain. There is always a temptation to link the Bangor and Aroostook with potatoes and leave it at that! It is true that Aroostook county produces more potatoes than the total of *any* potato-producing state, and it is true that potatoes contribute substantially to the meat-and-potatoes of the BAR, but it is equally true that this well-run, well-maintained railroad championed dieselization in the snow country, as well as CTC (Centralized Traffic Control), 115 lb. rail, and complete radio communications. Staff members and top executives are constantly in close contact, and it is not unusual for a road crew to all personally know the same vice president. Shippers are well taken care of with good service and the latest in rail equipment. In the earlier days of dieselization, the southbound *Aroostook Flyer's* E-7 diesel ignores the coaling dock at Northern Maine Jct. en route to Bangor and its Maine Central connection in July 1950 (at lower left). Below, a brand new GP-7 gets a close looking-over at Fort Kent, next to less-than-one-year-old BL-2 # 554 in June 1950. (BOGEN, BOGEN, LIBBY, COLLECTION)

Without a doubt, the *one* railroad in New England that had all the rural charm of a backwoods operation, yet railroaded in the best of main line tradition was the picturesque Rutland. All of its steam locomotives were built from around 1910 through 1920 (with the exception of four 4-8-2s built in 1946) and worked main line assignments on the single-track line up until 1952, when the final four Alco RS-3 diesels arrived on the property. In its heyday, the road operated neat, "distinctively Rutland" steam power that was the object of attention for many a rail photographer. The bucolic scene, at top left, is so typical of Rutland—an elderly F-11a Ten-Wheeler creeping up the weed-covered rails with the local from Rutland, arriving at Bennington in the summer of '49. At left, Rutland's doughty little 0-6-0 #106 rests from her chores in the Rutland, Vt., yard in November 1950.

It was the Central Vermont that endeared itself to me, however, running with big (for New England) steam while its neighbors operated their diesels. Only in 1954 did the CV take delivery of its first road diesels—two RS-3s—continuing to use its great T-3a class 2-10-4s on the hotshots. At upper right, a workaday vignette of the head end crew on a T-3a, going to work. Below, and at right, a roster shot of the original of the class, being readied for an assignment south out of White River Jct., Vt., on July 3, 1949. (BOGEN, PICKETT, DONAHUE, COLLINS)

How does one write about the Boston & Maine? It's sort of like giving a dissertation on apple pie and motherhood! It's been said B&M is the very spirit of New England: A Portland Division trainman coming to the rescue of a weary mother on a local passenger train and warming a baby bottle for her over a lantern . . . the satisfaction of school children who named B&M's newest steam locomotives . . . a Santa Claus appearing on *every* train arriving at Concord, New Hampshire. B&M is coffee, tea and milk open houses as it invites the public to look over the railroad's latest equipment. It is Professor Hooten of Harvard measuring over one thousand travelers in North Station in order to come up with the right-sized coach seat for the railroad!

Certainly in the transition years, B&M was the pioneer streamline train *Flying Yankee*, perhaps the operator of the most handsome of any 4-8-2s and, in my book, the prettiest diesel paint scheme this side of Chicago. B&M was also Moguls, covered bridges and red wooden cars. B&M was RDCs and an April 16, 1956, *Farewell to Steam* run to Portland behind big Lima 4-6-2 # 3713. B&M is a road to be remembered in better days.

In better days at upper left, E-7s pull out of Greenfield, Mass., with No. 57 for Albany on July 24, 1954; at lower left, a high-drivered Pacific wheeling commuters home along the Woburn loop, a few miles north of Winchester, in June 1954. At upper right, the pioneer streamliner *Flying Yankee* in Portland on Aug. 15, 1955, and at right, RS-3 # 1542 heading its four-car train through Wakefield, Mass., en route to Boston in June of '54. Why, who operated better looking RS-3s east of the GM&O . . . east of the Pacific Ocean?! (BALL, DONAHUE, BALL, DONAHUE)

Class. Pure Class.

First of all, was *any* streamlined steam locomotive more functionally beautiful than New Haven's I-5 Shoreliner? The princely locomotive was a thoroughbred at stride and the embodiment of elegance and the frozen image of speed at rest. Above, an I-5's unmistakable sharp exhaust is heard, and the eastbound *Yankee Clipper* hammers through Leete's Island, Ct., behind a no-longer-well-polished 1400. Still, the *Clipper* has a cachet of elegance about it—from stem to stern—as it always has since its first run on March 18, 1930. On this June 1948 day, it's obvious that Pullman Standard is delivering the new stainless steel cars, and with their turtleback roofs, curved skirting and Hunter green pier panels, the new cars are still unmistakeably New Haven! Inside, from their Yankee New England murals to the fresh scrodded haddock, brown bread, and baked beans in the diner, the train is still unmistakably New Haven!

At upper right, one of the racy aluminum and black bullet-nosed Baldwins scorches the Shore Line ballast at East Haven, Ct., moving the eastbound *Mayflower* in the summer of 1946. At lower right, turn-of-the-century K-1 class Mogul #373 works on the ballast train at Branford, Ct., in October 1948. Close to 44 percent of New Haven's gross revenues come from passenger service. That fine roadbed must constantly be maintained. (DONAHUE, DONAHUE, LIBBY)

There has existed a "great paint scheme debate" on the New Haven since the first Alco DL-109s entered service on Dec. 13, 1941. The consensus is that the railroad had, at one time or another, ten different paint schemes going for them on their road diesels! Usually the dark, or olive green with yellow (or was it deluxe gold?) pin stripes is identified as the "standard paint scheme." The truth of the matter is that the initial scheme was a Pullman green with imitation gold striping. Brunswick green with yellow stripes followed, only to be followed by Hunter green and deluxe gold (yellow). Then came the warm orange and Hunter green and then . . . In color, we can identify three of the schemes, but now, at upper right, there's a paint scheme not included in the ten variations! DL-109 # 0753 screams through East Haven, Ct., in October 1946, highballing symbol FGB-2 (Florida–Greenville–Boston) in a dapper gray and pin-striped "Brooks Brothers" attire. At left, pretty-as-you-please orange PAs head down the Shore Line through Leete's Island, Ct., with the westbound *Colonial* in June of '48. The train is obviously a "Penn job" to Washington, as evidenced by the Tuscan equipment. At lower left, set of DL-109s whistle by on the *Gilt Edge*, heading westbound in October 1946, between Branford and East Haven, Ct. Below right, the cherry for the whipped cream (or was it a cranberry?). In a picture taken with my first Kodak Pony 135 on Sept. 6, 1952, specially painted DL-109 # 0722 heads the *Cranberry* out of Boston, en route to Hyannis. On Fridays and Saturdays during the peak summer months, the train often ran with an additional diesel and fifteen cars—packed! (# 0722, BALL; ALL OTHERS DONAHUE)

On May 24, 1947, the first of fifteen new three-unit FA diesel-electric locomotives arrived on the New Haven property at West Springfield, Mass., en route from American Locomotive. The glistening 0401, 0450, and 0402 were spotted in the yard for the first official portrait—a stunning night shot. Several more daylight portraits were taken by the company photographer before the units headed light for New Haven. Below, the second set of FAs is pictured in June 1947, heading symbol OA-2 through Beacon Falls, Ct., on the Maybrook to Hartford run, where only last week, this same train was in the charge of an L-1 2-10-2. At lower left, Westinghouse EF-3 motor # 0155 hums eastward along track No. 2 with NB-4 out of Bay Ridge. She's shown in April 1954, approaching the west end of tower 60's interlocking at Bridgeport, Ct. At left, and in the evening of the same day, a newly-shopped "Tiger" heads local train No. 379 (the "milk run") out of Bridgeport for Grand Central Terminal, New York. This job works mail and baggage all the way to New York, and if you're in a hurry, you won't take this train! # 302 sports the new campaign slogan to "Give to the American Cancer Society," a public service effort that spread to the New Haven's entire roster. At right, pictured on June 18, 1956, a pair of Fairbanks-Morse C-Liners arrives in New Haven with train No. 181. As usual, she's heavy with head end cars (C-LINERS, BALL; ALL OTHERS, DONAHUE)

At first glance down the track, it is almost impossible to tell an EF-3 from an EP-4. Come again? At first glance, it is almost impossible to tell one of New Haven's streamlined 0150-class freight motors (called "yellow jackets" by the crews) from one of the high-wheeling lookalike 0361-class passenger motors ("streamliners" to the crews). Externally, the cooling screen on the EP-4's flank is longer, and that's about it. The EF-3 weighs thirty tons more than its lookalike and is pure AC. The EP-4 is an AC/DC machine since it is required to run over New York Central's 600-volt DC from Woodlawn into Grand Central Terminal. At upper left, EF-3 # 0152 heads GB-8 eastward through Bridgeport, Ct. She's out of Oak Point (New York City) with PRR, CNJ and LV freight for Cedar Hill, Springfield, Worcester, Provi-

dence and Boston. At left, and the general favorite of New Haven's electric crews, an EP-3 "flat bottom" roars through the interlocking and onto the Harlem River Branch past SS-22 at New Rochelle Jct., N.Y. It is here that the Hell Gate line (the "Branch") splits off the New York main line and heads for the Bronx freight terminals and Hell Gate bridge into Penn Station. The train shown is No. 177, *The Senator*, bound for Washington. Both shots were taken in March 1955. Above, three venerable EF-1 "Pony Motors" grind through Devon, Ct., with symbol HN-2 from Harlem River (Bronx) to Cedar Hill. Thirty-seven of these box cabs, Nos. 073–0111, were built between 1912 and 1913 and were still going strong in main line service into the fifties. (BALL, BALL, DONAHUE)

As the year 1954 drew to a close, the New Haven was operating 129 various electric locomotives, some of which had been in main line service since 1911! All were "distinctively New Haven" in looks, and were painted an olive-Hunter green, trimmed in the traditional yellow. The most recent electric locomotives were the ten EF-3 streamlined double-ended freight locomotives built in 1942 and 1943 to help with the war traffic. On Mar. 24, 1955, the "standard New Haven look" came to an abrupt end when ten flashy, black, white and Chinese vermillion GE ignitron rectifier locomotives began operations on the property. The flamboyant McGinnis engines with their rakish lines and big Barnum "NH" lettering not only looked different but also *sounded* different, with the roar of their cooling blowers. The crews did not take long to name the ten new engines "jets." Above, the regal # 377

approaches fast on track No. 1 at Burr Road tower in Bridgeport with the westbound *William Penn* for Penn Station in April 1955. Not long after the 370s were placed in service (and like anything new) they developed a few bugs, the most serious being electrical flash overs (fires). At upper right, the 377 is seen again, this time in the electric shop at New Haven, after a major fire and rebuilding. At lower right, EP-2 # 302 passes SS (signal station) 53 at Greens Farms with a westbound Springfield train. The structure supporting the transformers is an anchor bridge, equipped with circuit breakers to sectionalize the overhead wire. Any grounded wire would ring a bell in the tower and trip the breaker. The tower operator would then notify the Load Dispatcher at the Cos Cob power station for further instructions. (DONAHUE, BALL, DONAHUE)

When the shots on the left page were made of Pennsy trains entering Sunnyside yard in Long Island City on Mar. 17, 1952, the yard was the largest passenger car yard in the world, handling close to nine hundred cars every twenty-four hours! All eastbound PRR trains *officially* terminate in Penn Station, Manhattan but in fact must continue east, under the East River, on to Sunnyside for servicing. At left, the *Congressional* has made its sprint from Philadelphia and now, after emerging from the East River Tunnel, follows loop A under the Long Island Rail Road toward one of Sunnyside's seventy tracks. Yes, seventy! The maroon GG-1 is seen with the empty *Broadway Limited* on loop 2, which also swings around and into the yard. SOP allows a maximum servicing time of four hours per train before returning to Penn Station. All motors will be inspected and serviced, and washed on an elaborate 300-ft.-long wash track.

On this page, an immaculate Long Island H-10 steams into Jamaica station with a passenger extra on Aug. 18, 1952. To the immediate right, Fairbanks Morse C-Liner # 2401 heads into Jamaica with a train from Port Jefferson. The CPA24-5 was one of an order of four built for the LIRR in 1951—after permission was obtained from the court, the road being in bankruptcy at the time. The tower in the background is Jay Tower, the train movement nerve center on the railroad that carries one out of every four rail commuters in the United States. More than six-hundred trains pass in and out of Jamaica each weekday. (BALL)

The standard engine for all locomotive-hauled trains on the New York Central in and out of Grand Central Terminal was the T-class motor. Between 1913 and 1926, thirty-six of the electrics were built by GE for service in and out of GCT to Harmon and North White Plains—engine change points on the Hudson and Harlem Divisions. Above, and well inside New York City limits, T-motor #255 sweeps through the rock cut at Spuyten Duyvil with an inbound express from Poughkeepsie. At upper right, freshly shopped T-motor #278 heads the beautiful *20th Century Limited* across MO tower's electric interlocking, swinging toward Spuyten Duyvil and the thirty-four mile dash up the Hudson River to Harmon. Many of the train's personnel, from postal clerks to porters, are enjoying the warm spring air! The Harlem Division and New Haven trains continue straight on the far tracks, and at this point, Central's eastbounds are going the same direction as New Haven's westbounds, and vice versa! Observation "Sandy Creek" brings up the rear of the magnificent train. These pictures were taken on Memorial Day, 1954. (BALL)

Since 1913, all mainline New York Central trains running into Grand Central Terminal, New York City, have changed over to electric power at Harmon, N.Y., thirty-four miles to the north (west in the timetable) along the Hudson. The road's huge diesel and electric shops are located at Harmon, and during the days of steam, vast servicing facilities stood, including two giant roundhouses for passenger and freight power. The last steam locomotive "chuffed" out of Harmon (according to a reporter) on Aug. 19, 1953. Somehow "chuff" is not the right word, as others at Harmon, to see and photograph mighty Niagara # 6020, said it *blasted* out of town—in a shattering farewell, amidst horn salutes from virtually every diesel in the place!

In these right-after-steam views, above, the late afternoon sun breaks through the clouds upon the graceful flank of PA diesel # 4211 heading two mates out of the servicing tracks at Harmon to pick up the westbound *Ohio State Limited*, coming out from GCT behind a motor. At upper right, and on another day, E-8 diesels depart Harmon with the *Ohio State*. The view is from the railroad service road, with the train passing directly under the waiting room. At bottom right, an A-B-A set of Alco FAs cants into one of the many curves along the Hudson River just north of Peekskill, heading a meat train toward Harmon and, ultimately, down the west side of New York City to the St. John's Park Terminal near Canal Street. (BALL, BALL, DONAHUE)

"Upstate vignettes" might best describe the potpourri on this spread—at least for three of the pictures. At upper left, the March afternoon sun etches the contours of super J-3a Hudson # 54 backing her massive PT-4 tender through the leads from the Rensselaer Engine Terminal after receiving running repairs. Her unusual drivers are General Steel boxpock wheel centers designed for improved counterbalance with greater lateral and rim section strength. The year is 1953. At left, Lackawanna handsome Hudson # 1154 leaves Binghamton, N.Y., with train No. 1903 for Syracuse, carrying coaches and a Buffet Lounge Car. It's 1949 and pride is no longer evident on this 4-.

On January 1, 1938, the Delaware & Hudson had 375 locomotives, mostly 2-8-0 Consolidations. As traffic became heavier and more demanding, the road opted for forty modern 4-6-6-4 Class J Challengers and fifteen equally modern 4-8-4 Class K-62 Northerns, built by American Locomotive Company in 1940 and 1943 respectively. By year's end, 1947, the D&H was down to fewer than three hundred locomotives, with traffic and operating efficiency soaring due to the newer locomotives' greater power, speed and availability. Class K-62 # 302 wheels the *Laurentian* southbound through the beautiful forests near Saratoga Springs, N.Y., on Aug. 17, 1952. Far from the Adirondack vacation land, two of the huge Class J Challengers shove hard on the rear end of WR-3 on the mean Ararat grade in Pennsylvania in October of '51.

(BALL, BOGEN, COLLINS, COLLINS)

The Lehigh and New England Railroad took advantage of the peculiar "rock geography" of the region, serving the largest cement-producing areas, the slate belt and part of the rich anthracite region itself. L&NE, built in 1861, pioneered hauling cement in bulk and even designed and built its own special covered hopper cars for the service. The main line extends 187 miles from Hauto, Pa., in the heart of the anthracite properties of the parent Lehigh Coal and Navigation Company, to Campbell Hall, N.Y., and an interchange with the New Haven. L&NE ordered road-diesels early in the game, with the first Alco units arriving on the property in May 1948. Their dashing paint scheme of black and white stripes, punctuated by the bright "red ball" on the nose, is one of my all-time favorites. Four of the Alco FAs, now showing the ills of the financial woe that befell the road are shown, at left, entering Maybrook in October of '58. Above, arch competitor Lehigh and Hudson River dispatches hotshot OA-3 behind one of its mammoth Consolidations, seen storming out of Warwick, N.Y., en route to Bethlehem on Feb. 5, 1950. At right, Baldwin demonstrator sharks are moving through the Maybrook yard to pick up OA-1 on a trial L&HR revenue run to Bethlehem in June 1949. (BALL, COLLINS, BOGEN)

A pretty-as-you-please 6,000 h.p. lashup of new Erie phase IV F-3s bang over the L&NE crossover and past classic *MQ* tower at Campbell Hall, N.Y. The 187-car hotshot is out of Croxton yards, N.J., en route to Chicago. *MQ* is a 24-lever Saxby and Farmer mechanical interlocking tower on the Graham freight line which bypasses Middletown and Goshen, N.Y.—and commuter trains this time of day! The date is October 1955. (DONAHUE)

2

GOTHAM AND BEYOND

BALTIMORE & OHIO RAILROAD CO.
CENTRAL RAILROAD CO. OF NEW JERSEY
DELAWARE, LACKAWANNA AND WESTERN RAILROAD CO.
ERIE RAILROAD
LEHIGH VALLEY RAILROAD CO.
NEW YORK, ONTARIO AND WESTERN RAILWAY
NEW YORK, SUSQUEHANNA AND WESTERN RAILROAD CO.
PENNSYLVANIA RAILROAD
READING COMPANY
WESTERN MARYLAND RAILWAY

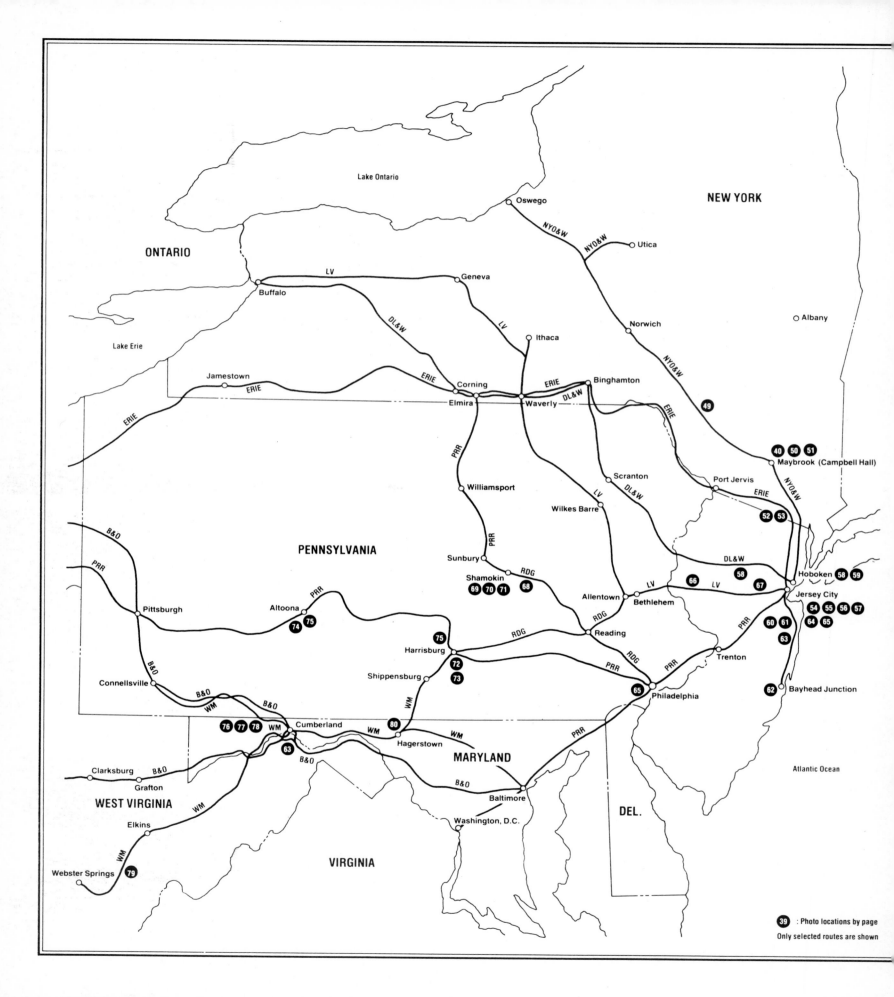

Lake Ontario

ONTARIO

NEW YORK

Oswego

NYO&W

NYO&W

Utica

LV

Geneva

Buffalo

Lake Erie

DL&W

LV

Norwich

Albany

Ithaca

NYO&W

Jamestown

ERIE

Corning

ERIE

Binghamton

ERIE

Elmira

Waverly

DL&W

ERIE

49

ERIE

PRR

40 50 51

Maybrook (Campbell Hall)

Williamsport

Scranton

Port Jervis

ERIE

NYO&W

52 53

PENNSYLVANIA

Wilkes Barre

LV

DL&W

PRR

DL&W

B&O

Sunbury

RDG

DL&W

58

Hoboken

58 59

PRR

Shamokin

69 70 71

68

LV

66

LV

67

Jersey City

Allentown

Bethlehem

54 55 56 57

Pittsburgh

Altoona

PRR

Reading

RDG

60 61

64 65

74 75

RDG

63

75

RDG

PRR

Trenton

Harrisburg

72

PRR

Connellsville

B&O

73

PRR

62 Bayhead Junction

Shippensburg

WM

65

Philadelphia

Atlantic Ocean

76 77 78

WM

Cumberland

WM

80

WM

63

B&O

Hagerstown

MARYLAND

DEL.

Clarksburg

B&O

Grafton

B&O

Baltimore

WEST VIRGINIA

WM

Washington, D.C.

Elkins

WM

VIRGINIA

Webster Springs

79

39 : Photo locations by page

Only selected routes are shown

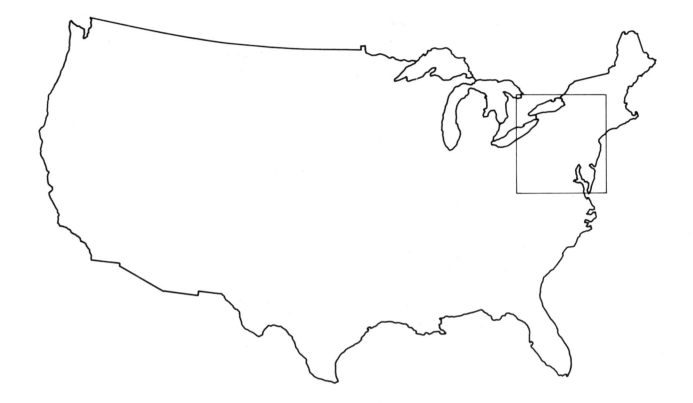

49 Roscoe, N.Y.
40, 50–1 Campbell Hall (CH), N.Y.
52–3 Spring Valley, N.Y.
58 Denville, N.J.
60, 61, 63 So. Amboy, N.J.
63 Middletown, N.J.
64–5 Elizabeth, N.J.
65 So. Philadelphia, Pa.
66 Pattenburg, N.J.
67 Bound Brook, N.J.
68 Gordon, Pa.
72–3 Enola Yard
74 Horse Shoe Curve
75 Duncannon, Pa.
63 Ridgely, W.Va.
76–8 Helmstetter's Curve
80 Williamsport Hill

SKIPPERS DO LOVE THEIR VESSELS even a double-ended, broad beam, shallow draft ferry boat. The salty, crusty old captain mellowed to a little conversation out his window once my buddy and I established the fact we had indeed written to the Lackawanna Railroad for permission to ride in the pilothouse of the 9:00 ferry from Barclay Street, Manhattan, to Hoboken. Armed with a copy of President Wm. White's note to, and accompanying release from, F. H. Cogan, Superintendent Marine Department of the railroad, we soon found ourselves standing next to the captain and aft pilothouse of the venerable steam-powered *Scranton*.

Our lofty location gives us an excellent view of the last automobiles being loaded, and the various deck hands and dock hands going about their chores. A bell rings, followed by the rattle of chains. The upper gang planks are raised, the heavy steel loading ramp pulled back. The gate is closed across the main deck while heaving lines attached to heavy hawsers are being cast off. Before *Scranton* is free of the bollards, a deck hand beckons us forward to the pilothouse. A gorgeous, 10-second long blast of the whistle bristles through the harbor air, and the captain positions the lever on the engine room telegraph to *Slow Ahead*. Down below, the engineer receives the bell command, and almost immediately we're throbbing out of the slip. White caps are bobbing out of the choppy water today from the icy dry squalls coming down the broad reach of the Hudson. *Full Ahead* is rung up on the telegraph, and the strong-running, tossing sea can be felt against the 231-foot hull of the *Scranton*. We watch the skipper at work.

Behind us looms the darkened side of Manhattan rising up between us and the morning sun. The rays that break between the buildings dramatize the tightly packed city; one senses the deep inner hustle of New York awakening for another day of work. "Quite a sight out here!" Manhattan's great din is no longer heard—just the inner throbs of the *Scranton*, the pleasant hard lapping of the waves, choppy splashes of bow spray and the ever-present whistles and horns of the great harbor. Tugs, tankers, oilers, barges, lighters, dredges, freighters, excursion boats, and police boats all share the mighty river with the numerous railroad ferries, seemingly filling every open space on the water. My remark about "roughing the winters" brings an instant, "No, it's a safe wheelhouse for the helmsman nowadays—steam-heated."

My buddy strikes a right note saying his ancestors were boat builders. The conversation is all the captain's now. "Most of our great wooden ships came from the New England forests; the tall, straight-grained pine logs for the spars, the tough oak for the planking. Masts must take the tremendous pressure of strong winds against the sails. Woe to the vessel with weak spars to be caught with shoals to leeward and a gale of wind blowing!" Then there was the matter of the hulls being strongly framed and . . . "No, I remember my Dad talking about the day he curled his fingers around the wheel in a March gale so they would freeze in shape around the wheel."

It's fun to guess when we're midway across; the jutting docks on both shores look the same now. Looking aft, the three red and black funnels of the *Queen Mary* in her berth are a beautiful sight, next to her, the two modernistic red, white and blue stacks of the 990-foot *United States*, both majestic symbols of the romance of travel. The captain tells us that over forty miles of piers line both shores! Ahead, the hodge-podgy industrial shore of New Jersey is quite distinct now, and the many visible smoke plumes mark the general directions of the various railroad yards and terminals. Southward—port side—is Jersey City and the Jersey Central's terminal. The ferry slips extend out from Jersey Central's almost medieval-looking green-copper-roofed building, which is also used by the Reading and Baltimore & Ohio, their passengers crossing the Hudson River by ferry to and from Liberty Street in downtown Manhattan. B&O goes "one step further" by operating their own buses via the Liberty Street ferry to four locations in mid-town Manhattan and one in Brooklyn. Of course, the B&O is not a commuter operation and contentedly caters to the long distance traveler—pampering them at that! A little closer is Erie's vast Jersey City terminal, reached by the Chambers Street Ferry, where twenty-one thousand commuters arrive and depart each day (and, I might add, with an almost flawless on-time record). Fifty-five trains are assigned to handle this suburban onslaught. Some of New York, Susquehanna and Western's trains also use Erie's Jersey City terminal. Off the starboard now is the New York Central's West Shore Terminal in Weehawken with its connecting ferryboats to 42nd Street, midtown, and Cortland Street, downtown, West Shore's huge, grain-elevator-looking pier 7 building with its five-story high New York Central System oval overshadows the ferry slips. The captain points out the ferry boat *Stony Point* passing off our starboard beam, the New York Central System oval clearly displayed on her tall stack. "She's headed to that slip next to the French Line pier." I can see the large rectangular white sign at the base of 42nd Street which says "New York Central System" with a smaller "N.Y.O.&W.Ry." initialed below. Like CNJ, Erie, and DL&W, the Central runs a fair amount of commuter trains in and out of Weehawken, with the ferries being the connecting link to New York City. The New York, Ontario & Western comes into Weehawken with only one train now.

This is a good time to point out that while the New York Central is the only road that comes *directly* onto Manhattan isle with freight trains, more freight is brought into New York on its West Shore line via car floats than on the direct rail route! Like most of the railroads serving Gotham, the New York Central has a veritable "railroad Navy" with its fleet of tugs, car floats and lighters. Other freight lines terminating in New Jersey that maintain sea-going connections are the Pennsylvania, Reading, Lehigh Valley, Erie, Lackawanna, B&O, and Jersey Central. The New York, Susquehanna & Western maintains a large freight terminal at Edgewater for direct rail car shipping to Gulf of Mexico ports. At times, the steaming Port of New York looks as though it is owned by the railroads! (I think it should be pointed out that Gotham, or New York City, comprises five boroughs: Manhattan, Brooklyn, Queens, the Bronx and Richmond, or Staten Island. Some independent communities in Gotham still go by their local names—Spuyten Duyvil, Long Island City, Bay Ridge, etc.) Nine trunk line railroads, fifteen terminal and short-haul roads which offer combined services with water carriers, make the Port of New York district the world's greatest port. In 1949, there were 402 rail-freight stations (157 in New York and 245 in New Jersey) with the bulk of the car loading and unloading taking place across the river in New Jersey. The "big story" to most people remains that of the commuter; the fact that over 600,000 rail-commuters enter and leave the city each day. Adding to this figure the over 100,000 daily visitors who travel to and from New York each day by rail, it is easy to understand why most Gotham area rail-photographers went for the passenger train action!

Slow Ahead is rung up on the engine room telegraph as we approach our slip; the current's push against our broad beam is felt in our momentary drifting. *Port Engines Ahead Two Thirds, Starboard Back Full*. We throw the stern to starboard. *All Back*. Time to leave the pilothouse to watch our approach. The screws are reversed and the *Scranton's* inners quiver as we head between the fenders. The water boils up as it is thrown forward. We wait for the first creaking crunch of the hull against the starboard pilings and the battering jolt back over to portside and again against the pilings. All hands on deck and dock go to work securing the *Scranton!* We will make the return trip back to Manhattan and then head for Chambers Street to catch a Jersey Central ferry over to the Jersey City Terminal and the outlying Communipaw yards.

Jersey Central—by no means one of my favorite railroads—is certainly a road that intrigued me more than most. In 1953, the railroad had to be operating the damnedest assortment of power of any railroad in the United States! I mean turn-of-the-century, high-wheeling center-cab camelbacks, right out of history books; locomotives now technically outlawed, yet appeared—from 0-4-0s to 0-8-8-0 mallets—at one time or another on no fewer than *fifty* U.S. and Mexican railroads and now, remain—survive is more like it—only on the Jersey Central. And the diesels that are taking over—custom built only-on-the-Jersey Central Baldwin double-ender diesel curiosities with cabs and controls on each end. Train Masters, all sorts of diesel switchers, Budd cars, Baldwin baby face diesels, but some of the most handsome Pacifics in the U.S. Jersey Central is a road of diverse eccentricities. Some of the color plates show a little of the color at Communipaw, including a shot of camelback #763 that hostler Benjamin Michaels "set up" for me between runs, so I could make a series of black-and-white studies of the engine. Another shot follows, showing one of the six Baldwin DR-6-4-20 double cab 2,000 h.p. units running on the New York & Long Branch.

More trips would be made to Jersey City and C'paw during the next two years, but 1954 would be my last visit. The last regular camelback run would be made on April 23, 1954, on train No. 709 to Dunellen, and Master Mechanic Gus Fertakos would assign engine #773 to the 12:42 P.M. midday train. No bunting, no brass band, not even a little sign—just an honest work-a-day end to an engine's career—and an era. Unlike so many railroads, steam bowed out on the CNJ in a nice sort of way. Sure when Pacific #830 headed train No. 829 out of Jersey City at 6:02 P.M. on April 23rd on the railroad's last steam assignment, it was on an appropriately rainy, gloomy day, and engineer Merwin Terry and fireman Joseph Greener sensed a bit of sorrow deep through 830's sturdy old frame, *but* it was also a time of festivity of CNJ's steam (CNJ being the short name for Central Railroad Company of New Jersey, or Jersey Central). Up at West Point during this last week of steam, camelback #774 was playing a role in Columbia Pictures' *The Long Gray Line,* a history of the United States Military Academy from 1903 to the present. To fellow stars Maureen O'Hara and Tyrone Power, #774 was nick-named "Engine First Class 774." (When John Wayne first saw the camelback go through her paces before and on camera, he looked at her and audibly said, "Well, I'll be damned." A re-take was promptly called for!) And while EFc #774 haughtily worked and hob-nobbed with the stars up at West Point, the completion of the total restoration of the "pride of the CNJ's camelback corps" Atlantic #592 was just about through. Taken out of service in 1949, this beautiful locomotive held the unofficial steam speed record of 120 mph for several years (reportedly running it many, many times!) and was now going to her final resting display place in B&O's great museum in Baltimore. #774 would return to C'paw to remain, alone, in the large Communipaw roundhouse for a call to handle a "Last of Steam" fantrip on July 12, 1954. A week later, #774 was placed—cold—in a local freight for what appeared to be a cruel and lonely voyage to the bone yard at Elizabethport for scrapping. As fate—and demand—would have it, however, the 1914 Baldwin would be yanked out of the bone yard for two more "final trips," on April 2, 1955, and September 25, 1955. Not a bad way for steam to go on the CNJ.

"Gotham and Beyond" depicts the great array of railroads within the commuting district of New York—roughly within a 75-mile radius of City Hall in lower Manhattan. Some of the prominent New York area railroads featured are also included in other chapters in this book, as their rails reach far beyond Gotham.

The rugged, splendid individualism of a railroad is nowhere better manifested than where the rails come to grip with mountains. The conflict is a basic one of conquest; one of producing ton-miles while breaking the back of a mountain, and almost every railroad is faced with a piece of "hill-climbing geography." The true mettle of a locomotive, the skill of engine crews, and the efficiency of the Operating Department all come into play in getting trains "up and over." And here is no-holds-barred railroading! Here is the railroad's finest piece of engineering upon which the naked, raging drama of climbing trains takes place. On Pennsy, 242 miles west of Philadelphia, high in the Alleghenies, the rails hug the steep wall of the mountains and swing around Horseshoe Curve rising to an elevation of 2200 feet at Gallitzin, Pa. Here is a four-track railroad that is seldom quiet, where the steady cannonading exhausts of up-bound trains on the 1.75 percent grade come from as many as four engines on one train. Here is where trains drifting down off the mountain are often hidden in their own brakeshoe smoke and where helper engines frequently drop down the mountain on the next track, brakeman riding high on the tender, watching for any potential trouble on the down-bound train. And here is the place to watch a westbound passenger or mail train climbing up the outside rail, overtaking the slower freights. On the Western Maryland (and this is the one railroad pictured in this chapter that is more "beyond than Gotham,") the story is much the same—their twisting rails encountering the Alleghenies' 1.75 percent climb six miles west of Cumberland. Watch, as WM's motive power—in multiples fore and aft —claw at the sanded rail, moving the tonnage over the mountains.

One final note: The tremendous interest in the anthracite railroads seems to be far out of proportion to comparably sized railroads and regions elsewhere. Perhaps this interest stems from the bleak beauty and history of the anthracite region itself, but I tend to believe the interest parallels the bittersweet economic growth and decline of the area and the railroads that served it. Though not "in the thick of things" as an anthracite road goes, nearby New York, Ontario & Western was nevertheless linked with the general region and certainly enjoyed a legion of devout followers far out of proportion to her 541 miles of railroad. O&W's strength did, at one time, come from the Scranton Division's link with the anthracite fields, but the rest of the railroad seemed to go from no place to nowhere. The road was financially sick and diesels, CTC and well publicized symbol freights could not save the Old Woman (her affectionate nickname). Her death came on March 29, 1957, to no one's surprise but just about everyone's sorrow. The appealing railroad was always a lady—a woman to those who knew her well. I'm reminded of an obituary written in *Trains* magazine "Because she was bad, so was she beautiful." The New York, Ontario & Western was a road of dreams and possessed a measure of glitter, magnetism, a bewitching sorcery that may have been based on illusions that transformed it or glorified it, or perhaps, just pity, or plain nostalgia. Certainly the Old Woman was in a land that itself was changing, if not downright dying, and this might have been the reason for the aura she had about her. I don't really know. Perhaps the O&W's perennial popularity can be felt in the pictures of her in this book; glamour in diesels . . . or is it an aging woman with heavy makeup and dyed hair?

One of the "thousand and one different vacations" that the New York, Ontario and Western takes you to is Roscoe, N.Y., located at the junction of the Beaverkill and Willowemoc trout streams in scenic Sullivan County, N.Y. After 1948, and after a steady decline of passenger service, Roscoe was as far north as any passenger trains would run, 137 miles out of New York (Weehawken). Pictured is train No. 1, the last remnant of the *Ontario Express* in December 1949, after its arrival at Roscoe from Weehawken. The first car is a heater car as the F-3 was not equipped with a steam boiler. (COLLINS)

The New York, Ontario & Western, known more affection-
ately as the Old Woman (or Old & Wobbly, Old & Weary, etc.)
was a railroad that could not live. With almost total decline
of its coal traffic and loss of its milk traffic and vacation traffic to the highway, the railroad became a bridge line with little traffic originating on its own property. Diesels and CTC
could not stem the steady tide of erosion of the railroad, and
when these two shots at CH were taken in November 1955,
one could sense that the once colorful line was on borrowed
time—dying, without destination or plan. The newly-created
slogan "Now Young, Out and Working" was lost rhetoric.

CH stands for Campbell Hall, N.Y., which was, perhaps,

the most important junction on the O&W in its final years,
providing access to the nearby Maybrook, N.Y., yards and
New Haven's bridge traffic. Above, westbound BC-3 is seen
with A-B-B-A F-Ts, pulling onto the O&W main, passing CH
station on its departure from Maybrook to Mayfield, Pa.
That's the Erie on the diamond, used also by the Lehigh &
New England, At right, F-3s and FTs bring inbound LB-4
slowly past CH station to pick up orders. The photo above was
taken from where CH Tower used to stand, before it was
closed and control of the junction went to the agent-operator
in CH station. By March 29, 1957, the agent-operator was no
longer needed . . . nor were the diesels or track. (DONAHUE)

Here we have the New Jersey and New York Railroad Company. The what? The New Jersey and New York Railroad Company, but looking for all the world like Erie, on any given morning in Spring Valley, N.Y. In 1938, the NJ&NY went into bankruptcy but continued to operate under the trusteeship of the Erie, leasing its locomotives and cars from Erie. Six commuter trains ran each day from Spring Valley to Jersey City—five of the trains departing within a little over an hour of each other. The single-track line retained a real rural flavor, and unlike the nearby four-track main of the Erie, operated in relative obscurity.

Right after Christmas 1953, December 27th to be precise, a buddy and I decided to drive over to Spring Valley to have a firsthand look at the classic lineup of K-1 Pacifics that I had heard so much about. I had always bypassed Erie in favor of other roads back east, yet I always looked upon Erie as being the "children's book classic": long semaphors, and fifty-year-old, high-drivered, high-domed, white-trimmed, polished and loved Pacifics, with their equally quaint trains of arch window Stillwell coaches. No one else could qualify. So Erie it became one morning, and my encounter at Spring Valley was everything I was told it would be. One petty disappointment was the fact I would have liked #2521 with her centered headlight to have been in the middle! I now look back on #2530 being the center attraction that morning as a stroke of fate, for on March 17, 1954, she ended an era on Erie, as fate would have it, the last steam locomotive to run on the railroad. (BALL)

It was *not* a white Christmas, 1951, nor a very severe winter, and that fact made the trip into New York on the New York Central and over to Chambers Street to catch Erie's ferry to Jersey City on January 25th a little more comfortable than usual. I had been given a new Kodak Pony 135 (which was replaced by an Argus C-3 within a year) for Christmas, and the Erie seemed a good bet for testing the camera. Erie's vast Jersey City terminal assured a hectic rush hour and a good variety of steam and diesel power to boot. (Erie was also a good railroad to try the new camera out on, for if things did go awry with the Kodak, it wouldn't be such a great loss—or so went my thinking at the time.)

The new camera has a Kodak Anaston 51 mm lens, opens to an aperture of f4.5 and has a top speed of 1/200 a second. Daylight-type Kodachrome film is loaded, there's plenty of crystal clear sun, so here goes! We have an ASA of 10—

At upper left, the lofty view from Terminal Tower as the evening rush begins. Looks as if 1/60 a second is not good enough to stop the PA, but look at the depth of field! At lower left, my very first pan shot—the subject being an RS-2 heading a train to Suffern, N.Y. From 5:05 to 6:05, thirty trains depart and a couple arrive; this number is doubled when you count the sets of equipment and engines that are backed into the station—one after another—so it's like being in a shooting gallery! To the upper right, and I'm losing my light fast, a couple of RS-3s and an F-3 are temporarily jammed up in the bottleneck, attempting to get back into the station. In a couple of minutes, and with less light to work with, I catch a PA diesel unit backing in toward its waiting Pt. Jervis train. Same shutter speed. At bottom right, the last rays of daylight glint off tenant New York, Susquehanna & Western's shiny Alco power and stainless steel commuter cars—good for catching and intensifying existing light. Time to head for the ferry. Oh yes, I did bring my black and white camera for the 4-6-2s—something I did not want to take a chance on losing! (BALL)

Generally, three commuter-carrying railroads are "associated with," or identified with New York City: the New York Central, Pennsylvania, and Long Island, the big three that come directly onto Manhattan Island. Across the Hudson, however, are equally important lines that reach New York City from Jersey City, Hoboken, and Weehawken via railroad-operated ferryboats. Singling out the Central Railroad of New Jersey: it gets its passengers to New York via ferryboat from its Jersey City terminal over to Liberty Street in downtown Manhattan. The Reading also uses the CNJ's tracks from Philadelphia, and the B&O comes on to the same rails at Bound Brook, N.J. All three roads tie up their power one mile east of the terminal's bumper posts at Communipaw, home of two roundhouses, a huge coaling dock, and an utterly bewildering layout of tracks. At left, a B&O E-7 and a Jersey Central G-2s Pacific head up the ready tracks at C-Paw, their next assignments being the *Royal Blue* and a midday train to Phillipsburg, respectively. At upper right, two Reading FP-7s in off the *Wall Street* head past for servicing; at lower right, the EMD "snouts" of both the CNJ and B&O. At lower left, one of Jersey Central's 4-6-0 camelback engines (also known as Mother Hubbard or center-cab locomotives) is posed by the hostler for its sunny portrait. All four photos were made on an unseasonably warm day, Mar. 18, 1953. (BALL)

I won my fame and
wide acclaim
For Lackawanna's
splendid name
By keeping bright
and snowy white
Upon the road of
anthracite.

So went the turn of the
century lyric about the
immaculate, legendary
Miss Phoebe Snow, which
Lackawanna created to
symbolize the cleanliness
of travel on their railroad.
The pictures on this
spread were all taken in
1952, when the DL&W
was 101 years old. Still
the shortest rail route between New York and
Buffalo—396 miles—the
road was rapidly ap-
proaching complete
dieselization with anthracite providing less than 10
percent of the revenues.
At lower left, one of the
road's smartly appointed
E-8s is ready to depart
from Hoboken on the
Scrantonian. #610 was
EMD's original E-8 de-
monstrator. At upper left,
one of the road's last active steamers, trim Pacific
#1119, arrives at De-
nville, N.J., en route to
Washington, N.J. At
right, a late afternoon
study of the lead unit of
an A-B-A lashup of F-3s
laying over at Hoboken.
(BOGEN, BOGEN, BALL)

Long after steam had departed
Harmon, North White Plains,
New Haven, Hoboken and Jersey
City, railfans could relish the fact
that there was *still* one last
citadel for steam in the New York
area at South Amboy, N.J.,
where Pennsy's celebrated K-4
Pacifics still took over from
GG-1s for the fast run down the
Jersey coast to Bay Head. PRR's
brutish, angular symbols of the
past absolutely defied the diesels,
handling tight schedules that
were seemingly unbeatable.
Those not partial to Pennsy
thought of the K-4 as just another
PRR plain-to-the-point-of-being-
ugly engine; those of us who stood
at trackside witnessing the over-
forty-year-old beasts in striding
command of their Tuscan trains
thought otherwise. One of my
fondest memories is taking my
buddy Karl to Morgan, N.J., in
January 1956. Karl, long an
"anti-Pennsy fan" did not appreciate the 7° temperature, nor
the chilling, icy wind off the water. He elected to stay in the car.
A sharp voiced K-4 was heard
and appeared, hammering hard
down the main toward us. Karl
joined me at trackside with his
movie camera to catch the big
Pacific with its colorful Tuscan
and gold P-70s. A usually unemo-
tional Karl turned to me and
shook his head. "Damn! What I've
missed!" Needless to say, my next
trips down along the Jersey Coast
would not be solo ventures. At
left, K-4 #3880 is serviced at the
So. Amboy engine terminal on
Apr. 10, 1956. At upper right, a
pristine Brunswick green G
heads out of So. Amboy toward
New York while below, a couple
of miles in the opposite direction
K-4 # 5473 storms out of So.
Amboy toward Bay Head in April
1954. (BALL, DONAHUE, PICKETT)

Color slides were for "scenes"—more for documentation at engine terminals, station stops and the like. Certainly, on the New York & Long Branch, a K-4 slamming over the Morgan Drawbridge spanning Cheesequake's fifty-foot channel was worthy of setting up for a 4 x 5 black-and-white action shot, or 16mm movies! Likewise any shot of a working steam locomotive on a *cold* day—assuring smoke and steam—was for black and white or movies. Once in a while, an exception is made. At upper right, an example: this early morning shot of K-4 # 3858 whamming through Middletown, N.J., with a northbound, under her mantle of condensed steam in April of '56. Diesels? Well, they were somehow part of the *total picture,* not a subject unto themselves. (More about that in the text!) At lower right, a Jersey Central double-ender Baldwin swings out of So. Amboy with homebound commuters in the summer of '56. At upper left, a new-comer to the Long Branch, Baldwin passenger shark # 5783, rolls into Bayhead on Aug. 18, 1957. At lower left, the switch is lined onto one of the ready tracks, as K-4 # 5419 brings her P-70s around the loop at Bayhead Jct. on Apr. 17, 1956. (WIDELL, BALL, BALL, DONAHUE)

One of the busiest locations, and certainly one of the best picture-taking places on *any* railroad in the U.S., is Elizabeth, N.J., where Pennsy's main line, carrying the heaviest traffic in America, crosses over the Jersey Central main at the east end of a beautiful "S" curve. In March 1954, on rails that are seldom quiet, three Pennsy trains are pictured at Elizabeth (clockwise from bottom right): Pennsy's two Baldwin-Westinghouse E-2b ignitron rectifier electrics rolling eastbound tonnage on the center track; 72"-drivered P-5a # 4732, making quick work with a westbound; and an MU train departing for a high-speed run down the main to New Brunswick and Trenton. At upper right, a scene not often observed on the Jersey Central, two of the road's massive M-3 Mikados blast the hazy sky over South Philadelphia, getting Jersey City-bound tonnage underway out of B&O's Eastside yard in May 1952. These heavy Mikes, purchased in 1925, along with five Pacifics purchased in 1930, were Jersey Central's newest power, up until the delivery of Baldwin double-ender road diesels in 1946. (PENNSY-BALL; CNJ-PICKETT)

64

Come one of those incredibly clear, shimmering summer days and it was time to put the top down on the car and go! During one such weekend in June 1955, the cool air was laden with the smell of honeysuckle and fresh cut grass. The wind was invigorating and the weather report called for "clear sailing" the next couple of days. Time to throw the pup tent in the trunk! Destination: Pattenburg, N.J., on the Lehigh Valley.

In what was otherwise a love affair with steam, I made an exception for the Lehigh Valley and Boston & Maine diesels back east. Certainly the subjects called for color! Three of my favorite shots of the Lehigh Valley appear on this spread,

shots that typify the picturesque and urban east end of the railroad. Above, and at precisely 10:50 A.M., two Cornell red Alco PAs race down the 131-lb. rail through Manville, N.J., with the Buffalo-bound *Black Diamond*. At lower left, the westbound *Diamond* is about to plunge, on that beautiful weekend, into Bellwood tunnel in Pattenburg. Earlier, the eastbound *John Wilkes* rushed out of the tunnel, heading toward New York behind a single Alco PA. For the rest of the daylight hours, there would be a couple of freights to wait for—with the thought of those fluffy clear weather cumulus clouds, with luck for background, and not shade! (BALL)

When a railroad's new diesels arrived on the property, the steamers were usually bumped to "lesser service," and in time, one or two isolated pockets, where maintenance could be concentrated. The irony—really a bitter pill to swallow—was the fact that the last holdouts for steam were usually the toughest assignments on the railroad. To a photographer, an obscure location to get to; to an operating crew, an assignment that "steam could easily handle"; to the brass back in the city office, a place to "get 'em out of the way"; always, somehow, a hell of a glorious end to a notable career.

On the Reading, one of the last "thankless tasks" for the great T-1 class 4-8-4s was to move coal—by pull or push—over the mountains out of Tamaqua and Gordon, in Pennsylvania. At left, two views of modern postwar T-1 # 2107 leaving Gordon, heading west with the hoppers on a chilly April 1956, day. Above, in March, 1956, really nothing more than transportation to and from where the steamers were, train No. 6, the *King Coal* prepares to leave Shamokin on the return run to Philadelphia. At the time, a "nondescript" diesel, now a vanished FM Train Master—itself as far removed from the railroad scene as the steamers. (BALL)

A few miles west of Shamokin, two of Pennsy's ponderous 2-10-0 Decapods battle along the twenty-seven-mile Shamokin Branch en route from Sunbury to the Lehigh Valley interchange at Mount Carmel. The standard train over the tortuous 1.3 percent ruling grade was 9000 tons, and like neighbor Reading, Pennsy kept steam on this back-breaking run until the very end. Our two performers on this cold April 1956, day are the 4219 (fore) and the 4243 (aft). These two I-1s have the combined tractive force of 192,000 lbs.—well over that of the world's most powerful articulated! (BALL)

Enola! Magic to a Pennsy fan, and certainly one of the most interesting railroad yards in America, located on the west shore of the Susquehanna River, two miles upstream from Harrisburg. Enola is the huge gathering place for electrics from the east and steam and diesel from the west. The vast yard is a constant hubbub of inbound and outbound trains, moving engines, and the continuous classifying of freight—eastbound/westbound, solid train/slow freight, preference freight/coal train—through electro-pneumatic switches and through retarder units down off the hump tracks. There is *no way* to show the size of Enola, other than with track diagrams or aerial photography! It is simply one of America's largest yards and goes constantly, around the clock, 24 hours each day, under its pall of smoke and constant din.

At upper left, on the Philadelphia Division engine tracks, a rare occurrence, with the only two Baldwin-Lima-Westinghouse experimental E3c rectifier locomotives alongside two of the three experimental General Electric E2b rectifiers. The stakes are high, as both builders are after an order to replace PRR's huge fleet of aging P-5 motors. At lower left, a "hippo" 2-10-0 Decapod plods past the eastbound preference classification yard hump tower after its tour of work and heads for the lead that will take her back to the servicing facilities. At upper right, an employee who apparently shared the feelings of many of us at the time makes his thoughts known on the

4253 cylinder's, shown passing the Middle Division cabin track. Below, at the end of a day, and toward the end of an era on the Pennsylvania Railroad, I-1 # 4616 heads westbound tonnage out of Enola. The date for all of these pictures is Sept. 4, 1957. (WIDELL)

Hindsight is wonderful! In 1955, '56, and '57 when we made our end-of-the-summer steam-chasing safaris to B&O country, we relegated Pennsy to afterthought—a grimy family of lookalike engines toting crusty hoppers on a railraod that, as we used to say, hauled ties in their dining cars! How wrong we were, for the few Pennsy shots I did go for are now near and dear to my heart. The likes of Horse Shoe couldn't compete with B&O, NYC, or L&N at the time, but *now,* what could compare with the mighty four-track main of the Middle Division running along the Susquehanna and over the mountains! Ironically, I've gone back to Pennsy several times for diesels, wishing it were steam.

At left, and on a glorious, Indian Summer Oct. 13, 1955, general merchandise drifts eastward, down Horse Shoe, being paced by a huge J-1 assigned to westbound pusher service; on the outside track, two GP-7s lead E-8s on a furious assault up the mountain with No. 14, a fast time-carded mail and express train to Pittsburgh, carrying two coaches on the rear end. At right, and along that "now beautiful Middle Division," an M-1 rolls the reefers along the Susquehanna westbound near Duncannon on Sept. 15, 1955, followed by an A-B-A trio of F-3s on general mechandise. At lower right, the Queen Mary! Would you believe mile-long Baldwin Centipede at Altoona?! (*Left page,* PICKETT: *right page,* BALL, BALL, CAVANAUGH)

To my way of thinking, the Western Maryland has always been a railroadman's railroad. This might sound a little strange, but consider the fact that the road was once figured into a transcontinental dream system of George W. Gould, at the turn of the century. Consider also, the road never really got into any passenger service to speak of—certainly nothing more than provision of basic transport for its customers. Consider also that "he-man Western Maryland" hauled coal out of the mountains to its own tidewater terminal and provided the shortest route from the Great Lakes to the Atlantic seaboard. Western Maryland was fast-carded redball freights, most of which moved during the days of steam behind examples of the most modern 4-8-4s and 4-6-6-4s in the country. In the days of steam, no-nonsense Western Maryland hauled the heaviest tonnage of *any* class I railroad in the U.S. over a 3 percent grade—usually with the boost from one of their most-powerful-in-the-world 2-10-0s.

The *Fast Freight Line* is pictured across the spread, moving WM-1 over the Alleghenies west of Cumberland in typically Western Maryland fashion—doggedly determined to get everything over the mountains as quickly as drawbars will allow! Aug. 23, 1952. (COLLINS)

OVERLEAF: A railroad's annual report from the steam-to-diesel transition years will graphically and coldly tell what those of us tracking down steam usually found out the hard way— how *quickly* the diesels took over! Taking coal road Western Maryland and its 1954 annual report as an example, seventy-four steam freight locomotives were in service on Dec. 31, 1953, along with four passenger steamers. Accountants' statistics show that steam freight locomotives logged 1,018,533 miles in 1953, while steam passenger locomotives logged 150,609 miles; steam switching accounting for 115,854 miles. In 1954, the figures were 102,918 miles, 24,725 miles and 29,694 miles respectively. A further check of the General Balance Sheet, Operating Expenses and Ratios and Averages graphically shows and "justifies" the diesels' inroads. All seventy-eight steam locomotives were retired by July 1954. The three accompanying views are from a better year, 1951. At far left, my favorite picture in the book, showing the lovely sweep of Helmstedders curve in an idyllic summer portrait, 2-10-0 #1111 doing the honors on the climb. At immediate left, a new set of EMD F-7s droans out of Ridgely, W. Va., headed east past the block station in March, while below, a spectacular May 8th day at Cheat Bridge, W. Va., watching 2-8-0 #784 doing the honors on the rear end. What a day to go fishing! (COLLINS, DONAHUE, COLLINS)

OVERLEAF: The Williamsport Hill pusher. Western Maryland Railway, July 23, 1953. (LIBBY)

FROM DIXIE TO THE MIDLANDS

ATLANTIC COAST LINE RAILROAD CO.

BALTIMORE & OHIO RAILROAD CO.

CENTRAL OF GEORGIA RAILWAY CO.

CHESAPEAKE AND OHIO RAILWAY CO.

CHICAGO, INDIANAPOLIS AND LOUISVILLE RAILWAY CO.
(MONON RAILROAD)

FLORIDA EAST COAST RAILWAY

GRAND TRUNK WESTERN RAILWAY

LOUISVILLE & NASHVILLE RAILROAD CO.

NEW YORK CENTRAL SYSTEM

NEW YORK, CHICAGO AND ST. LOUIS RAILROAD

NORFOLK AND WESTERN RAILWAY

PENNSYLVANIA RAILROAD

RICHMOND, FREDERICKSBURG AND POTOMAC RAILROAD CO.

SEABOARD AIR LINE RAILROAD CO.

SOUTHERN RAILWAY SYSTEM

VIRGINIAN RAILWAY CO.

WABASH RAILROAD CO.

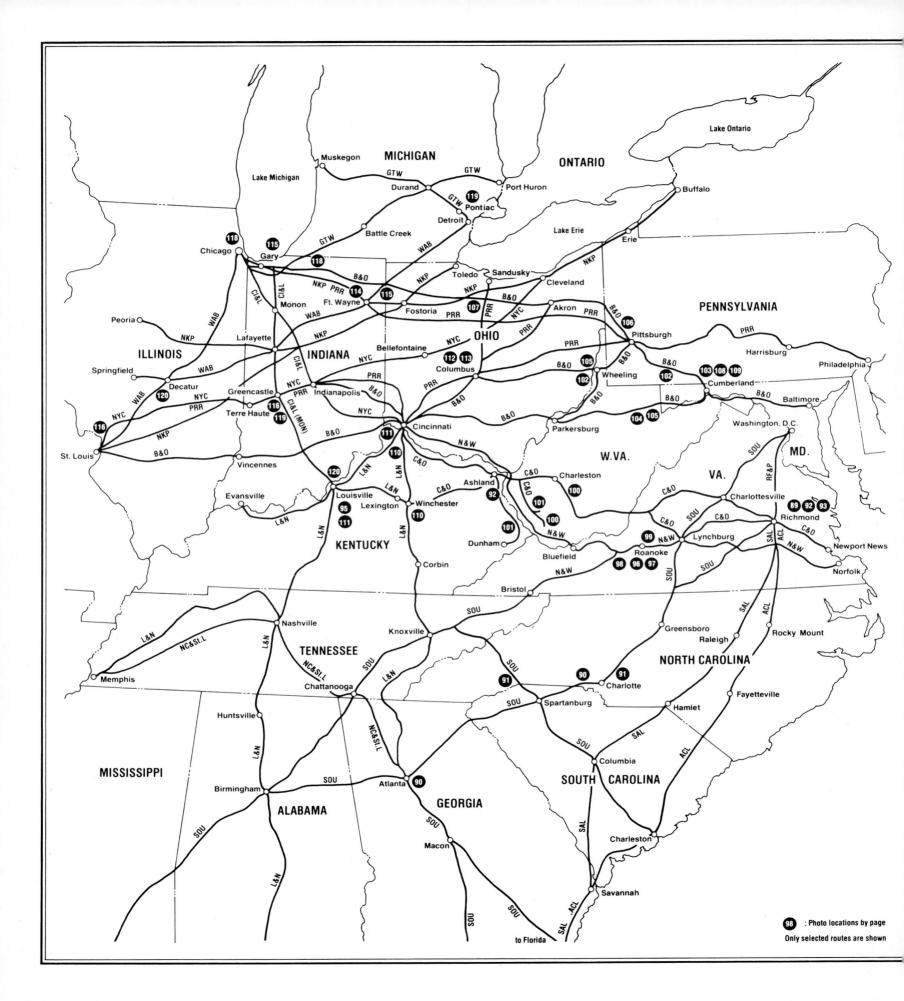

: Photo locations by page

Only selected routes are shown

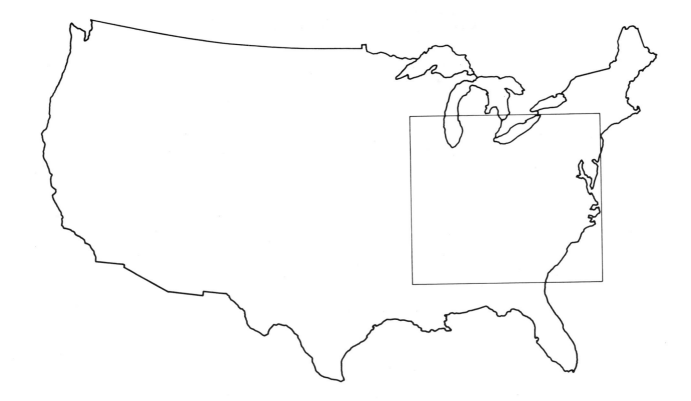

90   Gastonia, N.C.

91   Saluda Grade

91   Charlotte, N.C.

92   Ashland, Ky.

96, 97   Shaffer's Crossing

98   Walton, W.Va.

98   Salem, Va.

99   Blue Ridge

100   Handley, W.Va.

100   Scarlet, W.Va.

101   Peach Creek, W.Va.

101   Prestonsburg, Ky.

102   Bellaire, Ohio

102, 106, 108–09   Sandpatch Grade

103   State Line, Pa.

104   Cranbery Grade

105   Cheat River Grade

105   Benwood Jct.

107   Willard, Ohio

110   Winchester, Ky.

112   Delaware, Ohio

115   So. Gary, Ind.

118   So. Bend, Ind.

116   Mitchell, Ill.

119   Pontiac, Mich.

120   New Albany, Ind.

I AM A STANDER-IN-LINES, signer of last name, first name, middle initial; wearer of dink; receiver of chair, desk, tests, more tests, bed. I am soon a pledge—a rhine, wearer of pot, waxer of floors, shiner of shoes, washer of pans, waker-upper of actives, endurer of eight o'clocks, dreader of exams, hater of deadlines, receiver of paddle—and so goes the beginning of my first year of college. I am a reader of *Playboy,* lover of blanket parties, listener of Errol Garner, user of bum room, player of soccer, eater of pizza . . . and so we go forward, discovering our cultural and intellectual pursuits—Kappas, hayrides, waterfights, panty raids. I had always heard that fraternities and sororities are something that professors tolerate, independents abhor, freshmen marvel and parents could do well without. The fact is that DePauw is a school where tremendous emphasis is placed on the national Greek fraternal organizations (and incidentally academics) and pledging was (or seemed to be) as important as selecting a major—or going to classes!

All kidding aside, it soon becomes painfully evident that "making your grades" becomes the A number one responsibility in the fraternity house, and lengthy, mandatory study hours set by each house come as no surprise. It is also painfully evident that our house led the campus last year in Phi Beta Kappa membership. The grade leadership drive is to continue. It is also *painfully* evident that three railroads run through town (the Monon, New York Central and Pennsy) and that steam is still occasionally dispatched on the Central and the Penn. Whistles heard from inside a classroom, in the library or fraternity house, out on the soccer field, or during an ROTC inspection tell me railroading is still done in the grand manner, however sporadically. I am quickly compelled to devise great strategies to get to the tracks without being missed. I am a pledge . . . a rhine . . . accountable for all my time . . . available when free of studies, for pledge duties. Strategies are thought up, tried, some successfully, some not. Campus life is a world of compromise as it is, and the pursuit of trains just further complicates the already compromised campus life. I am a frosh . . . a lover of trains . . . an individual who is not about to compromise on *all* the steam running through town! By early October, the frost has replaced the dew across the Indiana landscape and the leaves begin their blaze of glory. All too soon, the sense of something ending is felt and no amount of cheering at football games seems to scuttle this feeling. The song birds of late summer are gone, their sounds replaced by the honking of migrating Canadian geese, winging high overhead in strong, erratic V-formations. Each day gets shorter; more and more leaves take flight and scatter, and walking out into the countryside becomes my temporary "escape." Out in the fields and along the tracks, there is a quality of presence that is almost chemical; a curious combination of electricity and drowsiness from the cool air, the tang of burning leaves and the mustiness of a quiet land. And have you noticed how still the autumn air can be? And how clear the distant sounds are? Perhaps this is from the fact that so many voices have been muted for the long season ahead; although I prefer to think it's from our sensitivity to, and awareness of, Mother Nature's final call that hails us out to be a part of the season's dramatic climax.

The passing of fall continues and I seem to be waiting for a suspended moment in time—for things to stop happening. I'm caught in a web. The grind of studies continues; life as a lowly pledge goes on. Saturday nights are heavenly, but when was the last time I heard a steam whistle on either the Pennsy or the Central?

It was on a too-nice-to-be-indoors Sunday afternoon in early November when a phone call came into the fraternity house asking for me. By coincidence, I was the pledge on phone duty. It was the Big Four (Central) operator on the other side of town whom I had made it my business to get to know. "We've got a 2800 coming west on a freight train . . . should be by here in thirty minutes." A quick and quiet swap of pledge duties was arranged, on the spot, with my gladly taking floor waxing for phone duty—*this time*. Black and white and color were set up for this one. The color shot appears in this chapter. This was the last steamer I'd see go through Greencastle, although I did not know it at the time. On a Saturday night hayride a month earlier, and under a harvest moon, I saw the last Pennsy steamer through town, J-1 #6447, heading west with a short freight more worthy of a 2-8-0. Her melodious whistle was haunting, but her skimpy train, the leisurely pace and her rods clanking on the pins all seemed to belie the fact she was nearing the end. It was heartbreakingly beautiful.

The coming of the New Year, the semester break, spring vacation—and a heck of a lot more free time—would, much to my delight, include more steam in my railroad world than I would have ever expected that first fall in Greencastle. In short, 1955, 1956, and 1957 would still bring honest-to-goodness steam operations where diesel dilemma or not, power balancing or not, breakdown and protection or not, bumper harvest or not, steam would still be found, routinely assigned to both passenger and freight trains. Illinois Central, Baltimore & Ohio, Nickel Plate, Norfolk & Western, Louisville & Nashville and Grand Trunk Western would become immediate objectives for steam safaris. Saturday trips turned into weekend trips; weekends, into an occasional three days—and trouble on the home front. I should mention that at DePauw [. . . well,] the policy stated in the catalog at the time says, "Virtually every student lives in University related housing. By tradition and policy, alcoholic beverages are not allowed and autos are restricted only to those who can show imperative need. The inevitable result is an excellent living experience concentrated in and around the University campus." I wholeheartedly agree with the philosophy and couldn't have loved any school more, *but* its policies did cramp my style when it came to tracking down steam! "Ingenious strategies" were called for! Oh, yes, I said New York Central and Pennsy steam was finished *through* Greencastle. Both railroads should be added to the list of steam safaris; you just had to know where to look. The old East College bell tolls every hour on the hour . . . 50 minute classes . . . ten minute breaks . . . think ; write faster! Time's up; hand it in. Did anyone else notice when the mellow steam whistles gave way to the harsh braying of airhorns. . .?

More than any other chapter in this book, Chapter Three is a diary of trips, forays—David P. Morgan coined the phrase, "steam safaris"—to document the iron horse in its final roles. It's obviously not by coincidence that most of the roads pictured are coal roads, burning in their fireboxes what they hauled. Because the imposition of the color plates falls into five chapters, there are exceptions to the very general theme, or geographic flow in each chapter, but apologies are not in the offing. In brilliant contrast to the coal-hauling roads which predominate this chapter, the Floridian railroads seemingly painted their diesels to match their flamboyant clientele and the land they rushed south to. When I was a kid, reading—rather I should say, looking through—Lucius Beebe's *Trains in Transition,* it was the second chapter, "The Diesel Dream," that really intrigued me. Beebe's ¾ wedge shots of those colorful creations out of La Grange documented the dazzling evolution that was taking place out on our nation's rails. Of all the new single unit starlets and multiple beauties that were pictured, the Atlantic Coast Line's purple, silver and gold trimmed diesels fascinated me the most. And when I saw Atlantic Coast Line's purple "in the flesh," it immediately became the prototype road for my first model repaint job—unfortunately a new Lionel New York Central series 2333 A-B-A F-3 diesel!

Meanwhile, back in the coal fields . . . Considering other railroads covered in this chapter, roads like the Chesapeake & Ohio, Norfolk & Western, Virginian, Baltimore & Ohio and Louisville & Nashville, this chapter should be on coal—"black diamonds" to the railroad man. Out of geographic and economic necessity, I had to "limit" my steam-chasing trips, while at school, to the coal roads serving the rich bituminous fields of West Virginia, southern Ohio and eastern Kentucky, and luckily for me, I happened to be at the right place at the right time for a change! Singling out each of these roads would be a joyous task, but not for this book. So I'll just make a few "capsule comments," since we're talking about such railroads as the Chesapeake & Ohio, the nation's foremost originator and carrier of bituminous coal, the road that traditionally carries approximately one-eighth of the nation's production of bituminous. We're talking about the railroad whose colorful President Robert R. Young ran a vigorous post-war ad campaign for coast-to-coast passenger service, proclaiming, "A hog can cross the country without changing trains, but you can't." And we're talking about a railroad that dreamed of, and built, perhaps the most unusual and luxurious passenger train ever conceived—from its streamlined coal-fired turbine locomotives to its vista domed diner-lounge observation cars. Why, a motion picture theater, library and stewardess-nurse were even among the innovations. The train's name was *Chessie,* after the C&O's trademark kitten, but the fluted stainless steel dream died (as did the goldfish in the train's illuminated aquarium) having never run a revenue mile. The road stuck to concentrating on better ways of handling coal.

The second largest bituminous road is the Norfolk & Western, with its rich abundance of Pocahontas coal in the rugged mountains between Bluefield and Kenova, W. Va.—the Thacker, Kenova, Pocahontas, Upper Buchanan, Tug River and Clinch Valley districts. This is a back country where in ridge-ringed valleys, tiny settlements are grouped around mine shafts and coal loading tipples. The heavy single track rail lines to the mines are everywhere, coming down off ridges, climbing behind "that hill over there"—much the same as on the C&O. Collecting all of this back woods coal, dragging it to the main line, and running it back to the classification yards is a back-breaking proposition for the railroad.

The best known piece of pre-dieselization history is Norfolk & Western's staunch belief in running a railroad with perfected steam power. I have briefly talked about this in the picture text, but simply put, the N&W continued to build its own steam locomotives in its own Roanoke Shops—and then go on to break all kinds of motive power records in the face of the diesel invader—way after most other railroads were dieselized! After the last commercial locomotive builder in the U. S. constructed its last steamer in 1949, Roanoke happily went about its business, full time, building steam. (Breaking my own rule of keeping everything in present tense, the last order by the N&W for steam came in 1953, for Roanoke to construct forty-five 0-8-0's.) No doubt about the fact that the ultimate in steam locomotive development came out of Roanoke.

A personal viewpoint: I am not an admirer of Norfolk & Western steam from the standpoint of aesthetics, but when it came to having N&W steam, *or no steam at all,* I spent plenty of time along the railroad. I drove as fast as anyone, along Shenandoah Avenue in Roanoke, racing the traffic lights westward to make that left turn onto 24th Street and head for the tunnel into N&W property. My heart beat as fast as anyone's upon seeing the huge roundhouse full of steam . . . and certainly my all-time favorite hotel *anywhere* was the beautiful Queen Anne-style Hotel Roanoke, whose lush green lawn spread down to the tracks and trains I had come to see. Why, Randolph Tower itself was worth the grueling straight-through drive—just to see the parade of eastbounds heading toward the eleven-mile 1.2 percent climb up Blue Ridge. And what experience-in-steam could top being out in the lovely country on Blue Ridge on a summer's eve waiting for, and then watching, one of Roanoke Shop's magnificent Js thunder up the hill—accelerating, yet!—with the eastbound *Pocahontas* streamliner. I loved the fact that people along the way could tell time by the "Poke," and it ran behind steam.

Back in Roanoke and across town is the Virginian Railway—a modern 661-mile system (including 138 miles of electrified territory) with bituminous coal accounting for about eighty-seven percent of the total freight tonnage handled. The prosperous railroad enjoys the second lowest ratio of operating costs to operating payroll. I have elected to show two of its unique electric locomotives in this volume, since its two classes of main line steam power are just about identical to C&O's huge Alco and Lima built 2-8-4s and Lima's massive 2-6-6-6s, both pictured in this book along the C&O.

Turning to my favorite in the east, the Baltimore & Ohio, it is certainly a major coal-hauler, too, although mine products (coal, ores, sand and stone) account for about sixty-two percent of all the tonnage handled. In 1955, the B&O moved 814,000 carloads of bituminous coal, totaling some 48,500,000 tons and representing about forty-two percent of the entire freight tonnage. Coke and anthracite coal accounted for another 2,400,000 tons or approximately 61,200 carloads. On the passenger side of the business, the B&O, like the C&O, made plans to completely revitalize its passenger trains in the post-war years, but unlike Chessie, it successfully placed in service several new streamliners—with the vista domes (Strata-Domes on the B&O) and stewardess-nurses that C&O only dreamed about. One of my most memorable train trips was on B&O's plush new *Columbian* in June of 1952, heading by way of Chicago for a summer of work and visit with my grandparents back in Lawrence, Kansas. After the station stop at Silver Spring, Md., and well away from the overhead catenary back in Washington, the dome was open for the first twenty-four of us who were waiting in line. This was my first ride in a vista dome. What really sticks in my mind is the summer evening in the mountains, and especialy Cumberland: At approximately 7:30 P.M., we swing past the vast yards, past the shops, the roundhouse and the big old Armour and Swift & Co. packing houses approaching Cumberland. The gleaming blue, gray and gold train eases over switches and rocks gently through a crossover and to a velvety smooth stop in front of the large old red brick and white trimmed Queen City Hotel and station. Looking down and out from the dome, it becomes apparent that Cumberland is a busy railroad town. To the left, an endless procession of hopper cars heads west; to the right and all along Park Street and down on Henderson Street, people are standing out in the cool evening air, standing or sitting on steps, watching the railroad. Everywhere you look, Cumberland is a city of flat-faced red brick buildings along, or overlooking, the railroad. At about the time I stand up to go downstairs and out on the platform for a stretch, a man with a wash broom and bucket appears on the dome overhead and commences cleaning every pane of glass. This fascinating bit of railroading, I might add, takes all my attention away from the *other* aspects of railroading that were happening in Cumberland. After a short ten minutes, we are underway. By the time we pass ND Tower at Viaduct Jct. (where the St. Louis line splits off west) the phenomenon of the darkened dome is quickly explained. Up front, we have a P-1d helper, booming away, heaving her cinders all over the still wet glass of the dome! I did not even notice her when she was added onto the train at Cumberland. The 4-6-2 blasts away under U.S. route 40 and under the Western Maryland. We quickly duck through the dense smoke under both bridges and now are hugging the mountains, Wills Creek on our left. We are through The Narrows. In thirteen miles, we slam past the helper station and Q Tower at Hyndman, on the beginning of our assault of the Alleghenies. As darkness closes in we are all wondering when the last corner of cinders will blow off the window panes overhead!

Now, a word about L&N and its 2-8-4s. In 1954, while finishing up a three week end-of-summer steam chase that would end in Cincinnati, we decided to head across the Ohio River to DeCoursey, Ky., to have a quick look at some L&N 2-8-4s. The L&N had always been an unknown railroad to me, and the 2-8-4 wheel arrangement about my least favorite. The combination of the two left little incentive to go to DeCoursey! Two factors came into play here: It was not my car, and there was really nothing to prevent my going. B&O's P-7s and Central's Niagaras would have to wait a day.

The visit to L&N's property turned out to be the highlight of the three week trip for me. At once I felt the deep, friendly pride of the railroad, starting with the yardmaster, who decided to give us the Cook's tour! Over at the roundhouse, we got our first look at Berkshire #1973 clumping onto the 120-foot long turntable. "They don't come any better," said our host, and for a moment it was as though we were looking over a bluegrass thoroughbred. She *was* beautifully balanced, and well, downright racy. She smacked of everything I love about a well-proportioned Northern, and yet she was a Berk. The big 2-8-4 was L&N's best in steam, and I thought to myself if Rock Island or even Santa Fe had gone for a Berkshire, this would be it; glancing over her rakish tender, I thought she might have been Norfolk & Western's fling at the 2-8-4. But she was all L&N, and for the moment it was time to savor the yardmaster's enthusiasm—nay, downright enchantment—over his railroad's charge. "She can make for quite a stew in the hills and roundabout." We stayed, and decided to end this trip down on the L&N. The yardmaster was right.

Finally, after my remarks about the Pennsy in an earlier caption, I'd like to make partial amends by getting on the record in so far as the J-1 class engines are concerned. During the steam safaris to "B&O country," not one trip was made without spending some time on Pennsy's Columbus–Sandusky line to see some of PRR's fabulous 2-10-4s! Sure, they were basic copies of C&O's T-1 (Is anything wrong with that?) but the strong "Pennsy look" about 'em was unmistakable. From the boiler front keystone, high mounted headlight and solid 16-wheel tender, the J-1 smacked of everything modern Pennsy was all about—and then some. In many ways, the J-1 was a compromise between tradition and PRR's last wonderful fling at duplexes and experimentals; I've always felt the fabulous J was really *the* all around Pennsy engine. Personal opinion, of course.

In a book of otherwise unpublished pictures, this color classic of Southern's graceful Ps-2 Pacific # 1344 departing Richmond's Hull Street Station is worthy of being the exception. The train carrying connecting sleepers is SR's morning local, No. 11 to Danville, in March of 1948. (LIBBY)

Not all photographs of the Southern were taken on Saluda grade or at Alexandria. To the immediate left, the dashing green-jacketed PS-4 is rushing the southbound Piedmont Limited near Gastonia, N.C., on Southern's busy Charlotte Division—a 304-mile stretch of double track running from Spencer, N.C., down through textile and tobacco country to Atlanta. At lower right is one of Southern's handsome MS-4 class heavy Mikes heading time freight No. 55 southbound, just east of Charlotte in the summer of 1946 At upper right, Southern's "Big Fifty" #5077 drifts down Saluda Mountain's treacherous 4.3 percent past Safety Track No. 1; her "squirls tail pops" signaling a hot, well-fired engine. The safety track leads sharply up grade over 1,000 feet into 60 feet of solid earth—enough to stop the heaviest runaway freight. The track switch is *always* lined for the safety track and is manually thrown for the main only upon proper whistle signal from the down grade train. At the lower left, and a change of pace from the Southern-in-steam, two Central of Georgia E-7s make their 6:15 P.M. departure out of Atlanta with the streamlined *Nancy Hanks* for Savannah. (C OF G WALLIN COLLECTION, ALL OTHERS DONAHUE)

One of the best railroad properties in the country—and certainly one of the busiest—is the double-tracked, only 118-mile main line Richmond, Fredericksburg & Potomac between Washington, D.C., and Richmond, Va., that provides the vital link between the Atlantic Coast Line and Seaboard at Richmond, and the Pennsy in Washington (the RF&P also connects with the C&O, B&O and Southern). At immediate left and right are portraits shot in Richmond on May 17, 1954, of similarly painted ACL and RF&P diesels. The ACL F-7 and F-Ts are arriving with citrus from Florida, while the RF&P E-8 is being serviced for its next run north. At lower left, a view of RF&P's last steamer, an incredibly handsome 77″-drivered Baldwin 4-8-4, built in 1945 and named after the Virginia statesman, *Carter Braxton*. The 622 is far from home rails and far removed from a high speed varnish assignment for which she was designed; power-short C&O is leasing her to help move coal west out of Ashland, Ky., en route to Russell on Sept. 30, 1955. Coal-laden hoppers will tag along behind the ten-year-old thoroughbred, finishing a career. Below, one of Seaboard's homely looking Mikes heads a southbound freight through Richmond in September 1948, viewed from the Broad Street Bridge. (PICKETT, COLLINS, PICKETT, LIBBY)

In 1941 Lucius Beebe's book *Trains in Transition* was published, complementing his earlier volumes, *High Iron* and *Highliners*. The emergence of the diesel locomotive—most noticeably and colorfully in passenger service—on many class-1 railroads was very well documented in dramatic "¾ wedge" action photography. During my youth, this third book of Beebe's was my favorite, and the photographs in his "Diesel Dream" chapter made a lasting impact on me, an impact that ultimately inspired me to write this book, "doing it again," in color. Beebe's black-and-white shots of E-6 diesels racing along the Florida East Coast, Seaboard, and Atlantic Coast Line conjured up a rainbow of railroad color I had seen only in print, in an EMD-staged publicity lineup of diesels at Ivy City yards, Washington, D.C., ". . . a new era with General Motors Diesels."

In 1955, my school roommate and I made a spring trip down to his home in Florida. Only then did "Beebe's Florida diesels" come alive. The FEC, SAL, ACL colors on this spread symbolize, to me, the dazzle and impact the diesels so quickly brought to the railroads. At left, and shot from the window of a taxi, a Florida East Coast BL-2 diesel pulls into the stub track at the West Palm Beach station with a private car off the West India Fruit & Steamship Company, a Florida–Havana railraod car ferry service to Cuba. At lower left, Seaboard's *Silver Meteor* is seen behind E-7s at Miami on Feb. 6, 1953. On this page, and my favorite of the "Beebe paint schemes," Atlantic Coast Line E-6s get the highball out of Louisville, on the *South Wind*. (BALL, WALLIN COLLECTION, WALLIN COLLECTION)

The understatement in this book might well be something like, "The story of the Norfolk & Western is that of a Pocahontas coal road with a coal-to-tidewater operation of Paul Bunyan proportions." When commercial steam locomotive orders ceased in the U.S. in 1949, and America's railroads and locomotive builders went wholesale diesel, the Norfolk & Western happily went about its business of building, and perfecting, their already perfected steam locomotives! Not since 1927 had the N&W turned to anyone other than their own Roanoke Shops for a new locomotive. And this is the story of the Norfolk & Western.

In the photo, at left, taken at Shaffers Crossing (Roanoke) in April 1956, the three basic wheel arrangements employed—and perfected—by the N&W are shown left to right: the class A 2-6-6-4, class Y 2-8-8-2, and class J 4-8-4. Taking this particular sampling, the 1233 was completed on May 5, 1944; the 2015 (a class Y-3) on May 14, 1919; and the 605 on October 23, 1943. Over a span of thirty-five years, 221 of the huge 2-8-8-2 Y-class compounds were built, the final version being the class Y-6b, the world's most powerful steam locomotive.

Norfolk & Western's arch competitor is the relatively young Virginian Railway, completed in 1909 as a super conveyor belt from its rich bituminous mines in West Virginia to the port of Norfolk. The two locomotives on this page are also in Roanoke, the changeover point for electric operations through the mountains between Roanoke and Mullens, W. Va. At right, one of Virginian's gargantuan EL2B electrics rests her 6,800 horses and one million pounds upon the rails at Roanoke. She was built in 1948 by G.E. Below, a single EL-3A jackshaft electric lays over at Roanoke. Standard operating procedure is to run three of these 1925-era motors in a triple unit combo of 7,125 h.p. (PICKETT)

A few miles west of Roanoke, Norfolk & Western's fast *Powhatan Arrow* whams westward through Salem, Va., toward Bluefield, Williamson, Portsmouth and Cincinnati, behind clean-fired J # 607 on Memorial Day 1956. The third (center) track in the background is 6,169-foot-long passing track, and the view is off overhead highway U.S. 11. Further west, and on level ground, Y6b # 2161 rolls 170 empties through Walton, W. Va., 50 miles an hour. This shot, though not a spectacular one, is the absolute embodiment of N&W—manicured right-of-way, clean-fired engine, position light signals, and that endless black worm of hopper cars. At right, and on Sept. 1, 1957, greyhound class A # 1233 bounds down Blue Ridge at a customarily fast pace, rolling the hoppers as fast as journals, wheels and track permit. (BALL, BALL, WIDELL)

"Best earnings in company history. Best operating revenues of $380.3 million were 25 percent greater than the year before. . . . Best merchandise traffic revenues of $163.2 million were earned for moving a record tonnage of general freight . . . coal and coke revenues of $189.3 million, second highest in company history, were earned for moving coal tonnage which was almost one-third greater than the year before." So went Chesapeake & Ohio's 1955 annual report, and so went the railfans to C&O's tracks when it was learned steam was being taken out of storage and placed back in main line service to handle the increase of traffic. Main line service—where it belonged!

After the ranks of 4-6-4s, 2-8-2s, 2-10-4s, and 2-8-8-2s had long since disappeared from C&O's great roster of steam, Chessie was obliged to fire up some of their stored locomotives for one last steamy hurrah! Coal smoke once again drifted over the New River country of West Virginia—westward from Hinton to Handley—as C&O's finest wrote their last essay in steam. To the immediate right, huge H-8 Allegheny #1624 digs in on merchandise at Handley, W. Va., on June 6, 1956, a full year after being placed back in service. Below, two of Chessie's true mallet compound 2-6-6-2s blast the summer skies over remote Scarlet, W. Va., in May of

...55, working the local mine run up the steep grade to Holden, four long, hard miles away. At upper right, one of the great 2-8-4 Kanawas works coal down the well-maintained track at Prestonburg, Ky., in the Indian Summer of '55, while below right, we take a close look at "Big Mike" #2748 at Peach Creek, W. Va. Blower on, air pumps throbbing, generator whistling, she's ready for another assignment. (COLLINS)

Baltimore & Ohio Railroad—was there ever more of a household name among railroads than B&O? The B&O was the first railroad to be chartered (on Feb. 28, 1827) and built in America. From history books to Monopoly, the railroad was, and is, I'm sure, the best known of all American railroads. To those of us who knew the B&O up through the end of steam, the railroad was somehow special among railroads; perhaps it was the friendliness of its people; perhaps the scenery it traversed; perhaps just the history it conjured. No matter. To the rail photographer, the B&O was purely and simply its beautiful, classic locomotives—steam and diesel.

Three favorite spots to shoot the B&O in action are represented here: at top left, mighty EM-1 #674 (re-numbered from #7625) rumbles over the bridge off the Ohio River crossing at Bellaire, Ohio, on May 24, 1957, with a "humper" bound from Benwood Jct. (Wheeling) "over the hill" to Holloway, Ohio. At left, a smart A-B set of FAs work Sand Patch grade on May 24, 1956. On the rear end and way out of sight, a mighty 2-10-2. On this page, Q-4 Mike # 4496 is obviously fresh out of the shop, making for an eye-catching portrait, heading west on the Pittsburgh line out of the Cumberland Narrows on May 24, 1956. (COLLINS, DONAHUE, DONAHUE)

A more handsome representation of power you will not find, in my opinion, on any other spread in this book. At left, B&O's 2-8-8-4 Goliath, EM-1 # 7612 works up Cranberry grade's twisting rails under her bituminous pillar of exhaust near Amblersburg, W. Va., on an otherwise clear September day in 1947. Later the same day, the graceful, *Cincinnatian* glides downgrade over the stone arch Tray Run viaduct in Cheat River Canyon (at right), heading east toward M&K junction, W. Va., on her daylight dash from Cincinnati to Baltimore. Pictured below, and in the twilight of her career, the classic steam locomotive P-7c # 106 (originally numbered # 5308, the *President Harrison*) lays over in Benwood Jct., W. Va., on Apr. 4, 1957. When this picture was made, the 4-6-2 was assigned to standby protection power status for passenger trains on the Wheeling-Pittsburgh line. In another month, the 80′-drivered queen would be further downgraded to work train service, and then helper duty. In another few months . . . Within a year after returning from this trip, I wrote 0-scale trainmaker Max Gray, enclosing black-and-white photos of this engine, with a plea for production of a model of her. One can always dream. (HARLEY, KERRIGAN, BALL)

High up the eastern slope of Sand Patch, three 2-10-2s lift a westbound train up the 1.6 percent grade and around the 6° curve at Hablitzell, Pa., in March 1954. The remaining sunlight catches the dancing steam, the leafless branches of the trees sketching bare, delicate traceries against the cold evening light. The lonely splendor that is the Appalachian Mountains is very much present. The train's three engines will be heard in distant thunder for quite sometime yet, as darkness rapidly closes in. The woods will fall quiet, Wills Creek gently splashing down its run. Soon the anxious spell will be broken by the savage assault of the *Capitol Limited,* the *Columbian,* the *Ambassador* and maybe a freight or two. Above, the setting sun dances off the contours of B&O's T-3c Mountain #5575 at the Willard, Ohio, coaling dock in September 1955. (DONAHUE, DONAHUE, BALL)

The first mallet articulated locomotive in America was an 0-6-6-0 built by American Locomotive Company for the B&O in 1904. After exhibition at the Louisiana Purchase Exposition in St. Louis, this new, heaviest and most powerful locomotive in existence went to work in pusher service on Sand Patch grade's 1.98 percent profile. During the years 1911–1913, thirty 0-8-8-0 mallets of greater capacity were delivered to the B&O for pusher service on Sand Patch. The tremendous success of these locomotives led to an order of eighty-six more mallets between 1916 and 1920, this time of a 2-8-8-0 wheel arrangement. In 1944, the B&O placed a final order for the largest articulated locomotives it could possibly accommodate on the railroad—twenty mighty EM-1 class 2-8-8-4s built by Baldwin.

A little over fifty years after the first mallet shoved a train up Sand Patch, one of B&O's great EM-1s does the hellish honor on the head end, leaving the pushing to a pair of Santa Fe-type 2-10-2s. The location is the reverse S curve on Sand Patch at Mance, Pa., the date is Apr. 28, 1955. (Toward the end of the EM-1's mighty reign on Sand Patch, yellow Kodak film boxes were strewn all along the ballast, standing out in stark contrast to the black cinder cover!) At left, the 7606; at right, the two "Big Sixes," # 6105 and # 6140, bringing up the rear. There is no way one can imagine what it was like to get a long heavy train up over a mountain unless he witnessed from trackside the almost agonizing steel drama of the thunderous struggle. (COLLINS)

At the close of World War II, the Louisville & Nashville had comparatively few diesels in passenger service and none at all in freight service. The coal-minded road continued to develop new bituminous coal fields in western and eastern Kentucky during and after the war and ordered the world's heaviest 2-8-4 Berkshires in 1942, 1944, and 1949. In 1950, the L&N ordered its first road freight diesels, and for steam, the future course was charted. A sampling of the newest, and perhaps finest, of L&N steam and diesel is pictured on this spread.

At immediate left, a blast from the whistle and all-business Berkshire #1976 pounds past, leading an extra south through Spring Lake, Ky., on May 17, 1955. At lower left, and in the previous September, "Big Emma" #1986 rolls *The Old Reliable's* red hoppers southward through Winchester, Ky., about to cross the joint L&N/C&O east–west crossovers. At right, on Sept. 22, 1947, one of the L&N's new E-7s lays over at Cincinnati's engine house between assignments. Below, the setting winter sun peaks under the clouds and catches L&N's FP-7 #657 at Louisville. This diesel has a steam boiler and is assigned as protection power for passenger train service.
(COLLINS, BALL, KERRIGAN, R. T. SMART-WALLIN COLLECTION)

The summer of 1956 along Pennsy's "Atchison, Topeka & Ohio." Every spring, Pennsylvania's straight-shot, 112.7-mile Columbus–Sandusky line comes to life with 10,000-ton trains heading coal north and ore south as soon as traffic opens on the Great Lakes. PRR's huge J-1 class 2-10-4s ruled the rails—that is, until 1956, when leased Santa Fe 2-10-4s showed up, pitching in, helping with an abnormal increase in traffic. Strange sight indeed was seeing a normally crusty PRR locomotive shining in black wash paint next to a traditionally clean, but now crusty, Santa Fe engine! Such was the case at the Columbus roundhouse on Sept. 4, 1956. At the lower left, J-1 # 6468 heads through an early morning pastoral scene, an hour out of Grogan yard, Columbus, the plow and furrow left over from an earlier era. Above, a magnificant portrait of Pennsy's fabulous J-1, heading into the St. Clair Avenue engine house, Columbus. (BALL, BALL, WIDELL)

113

At year's end, 1955, the Nickel Plate saw to it that their great 2-8-4 Berkshires were prominently pictured throughout their annual report—from a head-on view of #779 (the last Berkshire delivered) on the cover, to Berks handling fast freight over the newly elevated track in Ft. Wayne and past the world's largest power shovel, "The Mountaineer," on an Ohio strip mine. Of little significance at the time was a faint line drawing of a GP-7 that appeared in the report's inside front cover. Out on the railroad things were very much as the Annual Report showed. Above, several of the road's great 2-8-4s are serviced in Ft. Wayne, while at lower right, sister engines #756 and #752 steam hot on the Ft. Wayne ready tracks. At upper right, PA #189 bangs across the Michigan Central crossover, bringing the Chicago-bound *Westerner* to its station stop at Gary on Apr. 2, 1955. On that 1955 Annual Report, the outline of a PA diesel appeared at the bottom of the front cover, under the 779. (WALLIN, VAN DUSEN, WALLIN)

During the spring of 1953, the first of 164 new GP-7 diesel locomotives started to arrive on New York Central's property. This huge locomotive order cost $27,500,000 and received much publicity in the business and financial world. Obviously, as the diesels were delivered, steam assignments were scratched, and by year's end 1954, all steam had vanished off the Central's rails east of Cleveland. Nine of the new arriving diesels even replaced the Cleveland Union Terminal electrics that had heretofore been used to keep steam out of Cleveland Union Terminal. Steam was being vanquished as fast as La Grange could produce, and Ohio, Indiana and Illinois soon became steam's last stronghold on the Central. Three of the four trains shown are random samplings of trains that drew steam in the spring of 1954. The shots are "trophies" of sorts, as by then, tracking down what steam locomotives were running where and when—and then photographing them—became exceedingly difficult. At immediate left, an L-2a Mohawk is dispatched west out of Indianapolis to Mattoon, Ill., on general merchandise. The train is pictured in the afternoon, a few miles east of Greencastle, Ind. Below, it's spring vacation and the *Southwestern Limited* makes a flag stop at Greencastle for some fraternity brothers and a girl friend, among others in the picture, heading for points east. On the other side of town, over on Locust Street, Pennsy's *Penn Texas* is making its simultaneous flag stop for students heading east. At lower left, J-1b Hudson #5204 shows the world she can still run like hell. Moving an extra, carded as Second No. 446, well over the posted 79 mph limit, she's a few hours off schedule. That she's running at all is due to a diesel breakdown. I was able to get this picture thanks to a way-too-early-in-the-morning phone call from the NYC operator at Greencastle. At far upper left, L-2c Mohawk #2922 shows us the glory of steam in the wintertime, heading east near Mitchell, Ill., in February 1954.

It's interesting to note that at the very close of steam operations, New York Central found it practical, or fashionable, to get rid of the newer steam power first, keeping older locomotives out on the railroad. #5402 was built in 1927, while look-alike freight counterparts 2873 and 2922 were built two years later—all three being American Locomotive products. (BALL)

Too often we think of the Grand Trunk Western as being the "Canadian National in the U.S." True, the Grand Trunk Western is the wholly-owned U.S. subsidiary of the CNR, but over its 974 miles of railroad in Michigan, Indiana, and Illinois run some very unique-to-the-States motive power. Take, for instance, the 5630 and the 6328 (above) facing us at the Pontiac, Mich., roundhouse. The 5630 is pure U.S. Built by Baldwin in 1929, this K-4-b Pacific is uniquely Grand Trunk Western, not CNR. As for the 6328, she was built by American Locomotive in 1942, and though "similar" to CNR's Canadian-built 4-8-4s, she still has a distinctly U.S.A.

look about her. Both engines are pictured on a quiet Sunday afternoon in July 1958, waiting for tomorrow morning's commuter rush. At upper left, two new phase IV F-3s back through the west side yard at South Bend, Ind., to tie on to Port Huron-bound tonnage on Feb. 5, 1949. At immediate left, Grand Trunk Western's *Mapleleaf* departs Chicago on June 21, 1947 behind U-4-b #6408. The six streamlined U-4-b Northerns were the notable Canadian-looking exceptions to Grand Trunk Western's roster; they were built by Lima in 1938 to match the Montreal-built U-4-as on the CNR. (VAN DUSEN, KERRIGAN, DONAHUE)

We close with two late afternoon, late fall ¾ action portraits; above, Wabash extra 554A east, heading through Hull, Ill. (for some reason, the railroad calls it Hulls!), out of Hannibal, bound for Decatur and Detroit. The lead unit heading FAs and an F-7 is the last Train Master delivered to the Wabash, complete with lowered front platform and steps. At right, Monon's pretty little train No. 5, *The Thoroughbred* speeding south of Borden, Ind., nearing its Louisville destination. (WALLIN, R. T. SMART-WALLIN COLLECTION)

4
MAIN LINES OF MID-AMERICA

ATCHISON, TOPEKA AND SANTA FE RAILWAY CO.

BALTIMORE & OHIO RAILROAD CO.

CHESAPEAKE AND OHIO RAILWAY CO.

CHICAGO & EASTERN ILLINOIS RAILROAD

CHICAGO AND NORTH WESTERN RAILWAY

CHICAGO, BURLINGTON & QUINCY RAILROAD

CHICAGO GREAT WESTERN RAILWAY

CHICAGO, MILWAUKEE, ST. PAUL AND PACIFIC RAILROAD

CHICAGO NORTH SHORE AND MILWAUKEE RAILWAY

CHICAGO, ROCK ISLAND AND PACIFIC RAILROAD CO.

CHICAGO SOUTH SHORE AND SOUTH BEND RAILROAD

DULUTH, MISSABE & IRON RANGE RAILWAY

ERIE RAILROAD

GULF, MOBILE AND OHIO RAILROAD

ILLINOIS CENTRAL RAILROAD

KANSAS CITY SOUTHERN LINES

MINNEAPOLIS, ST. PAUL & SAULT STE. MARIE RAILROAD CO.
(SOO LINE RAILROAD)

MISSOURI-KANSAS-TEXAS RAILROAD CO.

MISSOURI PACIFIC LINES

NEW YORK CENTRAL SYSTEM

NEW YORK, CHICAGO AND ST. LOUIS RAILROAD

PENNSYLVANIA RAILROAD

PERE MARQUETTE (C & O RY.)

ST. LOUIS-SAN FRANCISCO RAILWAY CO.

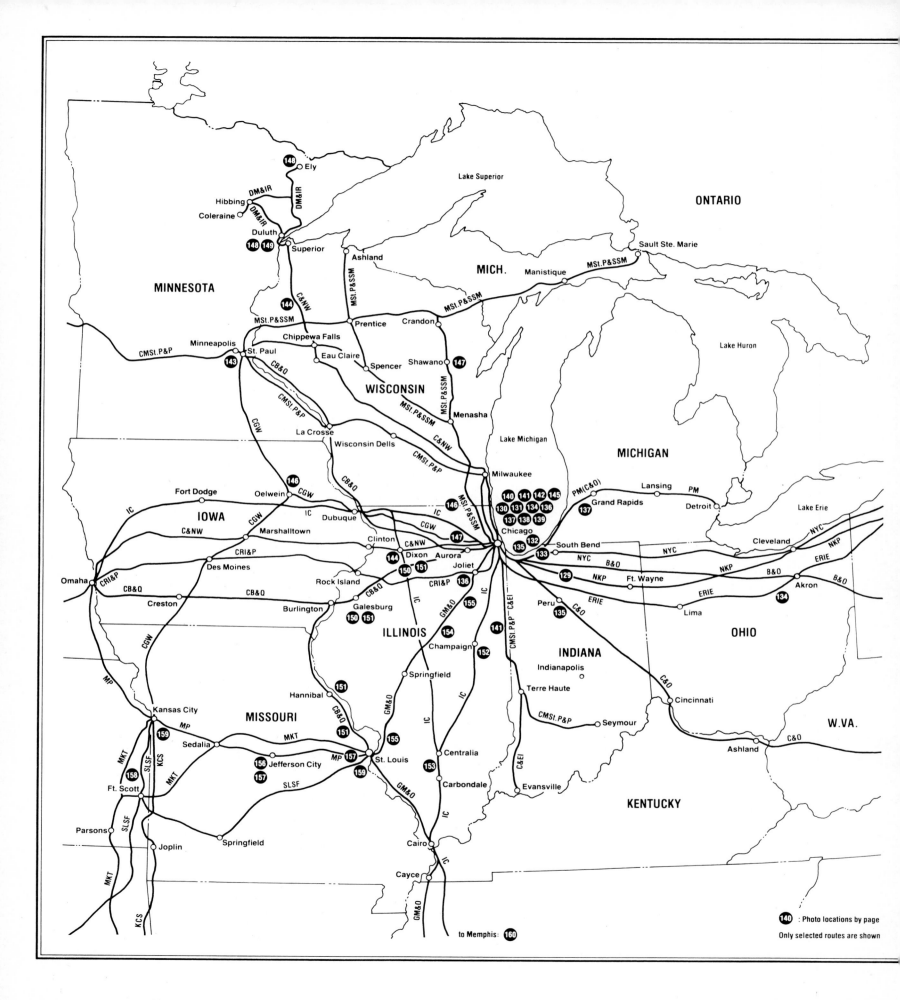

ONTARIO

Lake Superior

MICH.

Lake Huron

Lake Michigan

MICHIGAN

Lake Erie

OHIO

W.VA.

KENTUCKY

MINNESOTA

WISCONSIN

IOWA

ILLINOIS

INDIANA

MISSOURI

Ely 148

Hibbing
Coleraine
DM&IR
DM&IR
DM&IR
Duluth
148 149
Superior
Ashland
MSt.P&SSM
Sault Ste. Marie
Manistique
MSt.P&SSM

144
C&NW
MSt.P&SSM
Prentice
Crandon
MSt.P&SSM

Chippewa Falls
Eau Claire
Spencer
Shawano 147

CMSt.P&P
Minneapolis
St. Paul
143
CB&Q
MSt.P&SSM
MSt.P&SSM
C&NW
Menasha

CGW
CMSt.P&P
La Crosse
Wisconsin Dells
C&NW
CMSt.P&P
Milwaukee

Fort Dodge
Oelwein
146
CGW
IC
Dubuque
CB&Q
IC
146
MSt.P&SSM
Lansing
PM
PM(C&O)
Grand Rapids
137
Detroit

IC
C&NW
Marshalltown
CGW
CGW
Clinton
CGW
C&NW
Dixon
Aurora
144
150 151
Joliet
147
140 141 142 145
130 131 134 136
137 138 139
Chicago
132
135
133
South Bend
NYC
Cleveland
NYC
NKP
ERIE
B&O

CRI&P
Des Moines
CRI&P
Rock Island
CB&Q
CRI&P
136
IC
129
NKP
Ft. Wayne
B&O
NYC
NKP
ERIE
B&O
Akron 134

Omaha
CRI&P
CB&Q
Creston
CB&Q
Burlington
Galesburg
150 151
155
GM&O
141
CMSt.P&P C&EI
Peru
135
C&O
ERIE
Lima

MP
CGW
ILLINOIS
154
Champaign
152
IC
Indianapolis
INDIANA

151
Hannibal
CB&Q
Springfield
Terre Haute
CMSt.P&P
Seymour
Cincinnati

Kansas City
MP
MKT
159
Sedalia
MKT
156 Jefferson City
157
MP 157
151
155
St. Louis
153
Centralia
GM&O
IC
C&EI
C&O
Ashland

158
Ft. Scott
SLSF
KCS
MKT
159
Carbondale
Evansville

MISSOURI
Parsons
SLSF
MKT
KCS
Joplin
Springfield
SLSF
Cairo
IC
GM&O

Cayce

to Memphis: 160

140 : Photo locations by page

Only selected routes are shown

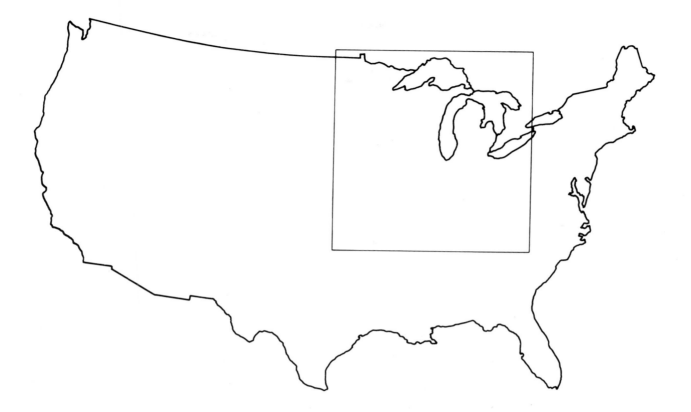

129 Mentone, Ind.

134 Creston, Ohio

135 Gary, Ind.

132–33 Michigan City, Ind.

132, 140 Evanston, Ill.

131 Englewood, Ill.

137 Grand Rapids, Mich.

140, 141 West Lake Forest, Ill.

141 Webster, Ill.

141 Techny, Ill.

144 Nelson, Ill.

144 Tuscobia, Wisc.

145 Geneva, Ill.

146 Antioch, Ill.

147 St. Charles, Ill.

147 Shawano, Wisc.

148–49 Proctor, Hill

150–51 Galesburg, Ill.

151 Elsberry, Mo.

150–51 Mendota, Ill.

152–53 DuQuoin, Ill.

153 Carbondale, Ill.

154 Lincoln, Ill.

155 Dwight, Ill.

155 Brighton, Ill.

157 Kirkwood, Mo.

158 Hillsdale, Ks.

As surely as all roads lead to Rome, the main lines of mid-America lead to Chicago. We're talking about a city within who's limits lie 7,720 track miles, out of which 3,036 are mainline; we're talking about twenty-two major carriers, seven belt, or terminal railroads, eight industrial lines and two heavy duty electric lines (some might want to add the Chicago, Aurora & Elgin as a third). At any given moment, approximately 1,100 locomotives are pushing, pulling, standing within the confines of Chicago; 50,000 freight cars can be found here—inbound, outbound, in yards, on riptracks, on industry sidings. As for passenger trains, Chicago has no peer. Every fifty-one seconds, a passenger train arrives or departs, an average of 3,600 passenger cars are within city limits at any given time! Mail and express have *not* been included in these figures, but the volume of this traffic is huge. No matter where a particular trunk line railroad comes from, or goes to, you can bet it will come in contact—somehow, someplace—with Chicago. (I immediately think of the fact that the *20th Century Limited* and *Broadway Limited* from New York cross paths with the *Golden State Limited* from California before they even get into Chicago. Of course, I'm talking about Englewood, and I forgot to add the *Nickel Plate Limited* to this entanglement!)

Chicago is the Baltimore & Ohio and Chicago & North Western bridging over the Burlington, the GM&O and the Pennsy. Chicago is the mighty Illinois Central racing the little Chicago, South Shore & South Bend toward Kensington—at the same speed yet! Chicago is railroad stations, like Dearborn, where Wabash's *Blue Bird* mingles with C&EI's *Meadowlark* and *Whippoorwill*, where Erie's two-toned green E-8s meet Grand Trunk Western's two-toned green 4-8-4s, and unobtrusive Monon eases its little diesel-powered Louisville and Indianapolis trains in amongst Santa Fe's long and dazzling transcontinental streamliners. And, let's not forget to throw in Chicago & Western Indiana's almost unknown commuter trains that burble in and out of Dearborn each day on their runs to and from Dalton. Mind you, I'm talking only about Dearborn Station! Why, there's also Union Station, Central Station, La Salle Station, Grand Central and Chicago & North Western Terminal. To complete the passenger picture, mention should be made of IC's suburban electric terminal at Randolph Street and South Shore's nearby terminus, where a total of 482 trains head in and out each day! And finally, perhaps the railroad with the most convenient access into Chicago—certainly the most centralized—is the Chicago, North Shore & Milwaukee, whose electric operations change from pole trolley to third-rail at Howard Street, Evanston, permitting their high speed Milwaukee trains to operate over the Chicago Transit Authority's rails right into the downtown Loop.

On the freight side of things, Chicago can deservedly boast of its 160 freight yards and 275 freight stations, for out of this maze of trackage, over 2,500 freight trains arrive and depart each day. This staggering figure can best be illustrated by picturing one-tenth of all the nation's freight trains operating throughout Chicago each day! A typical large yard in Chicago is the Belt Railway of Chicago's four-mile-long clearing yard owned by twelve of the railroads coming into Chicago. On any given day, well over 5,000 freight cars will originate, terminate, or pass through this yard, and at any given time, transfer runs can be seen arriving and departing, half of the runs being railroads other than the 12 ownership roads. There is good reason for the fact that Chicago appears in the corporate titles of over thirty-one railroads.

Of all the railroads coming to (or is it leaving from?) Chicago, two stand out in my opinion as being the all-around most colorful, especially in terms of neck and neck down-to-the-last-revenue-passenger performance. Of course, I'm referring to the Milwaukee Road and the Chicago & North Western. I've cited some dates and statistics in the picture captions, but I'm reminded of the late John W. Barriger's statement that "The super railroad is a route so intensively developed that maximum sized freight and passenger trains can cross entire engine districts without consequential intermediate speed restrictions." Well, between Western Avenue in Chicago and Kelley's Cut at the Milwaukee city limits, Milwaukee's 100 mph *Hiawathas* come close to being the absolute manifestation of Barriger's super railroad, running between both locations without applying the air! The greatest single contributing factor toward making this kind of running possible is the carefully calculated super elevation of the outer rail on curves, which the Milwaukee and the C&NW have perfected. In Milwaukee's case, the super elevation was increased from 2½" to 3½" with the coming of the lightweight streamlined *Hiawatha* trains. Curves were straightened out to a minimum of one degree, or 5,730 feet in radius. (Can you imagine what passengers must have thought, back in 1935, looking out the windows of their train and seeing the maintenance-of-way men erecting those legendary yellow and black *Reduce-Speed-to-90* signs!)

There are "heroes and villains" to every story and certainly the *Hiawatha* story is no exception. The track raiser taking a sight on the outer rail along Milwaukee's main and carefully watching the power jack raise the rail to the precise height (the railroad raised it again, this time to 4") helped make the 100 mph plus speeds possible—but for both steam and diesel! Steam reigned and made headlines with the popular *Hiawathas* in the '30s and early '40s, but when a couple of lonely pairs of diesels arrived from Alco and EMD—and did what steam did, and better—*they* were the villains in the tale of the almost legendary *Hiawathas*. Almost imperceptibly, the diesels quickly moved in and took over while too many of us were left at trackside, comparing paint schemes in the wake of steam.

In the early '50s on the Illinois Central, the story was a simple one: colorfully painted diesels had taken over on the streamliners, while just-plain-black diesels had taken over on switching and transfer runs where smoke could be a problem or sparks could potentially blow a customer off the map. For steam, on the freight side of business, the future was bright. The railroad began an ambitious $9 million equipment purchase program in 1951, and President Wayne A. Johnston saw to it that steam was succinctly placed in proper perspective in the PR release announcing the new equipment program, which said: "The Illinois Central is primarily a coal-transporting and a coal-burning railroad, and all our freight trains are powered with coal-burning locomotives." Johnston continued, "Certain conditions, however, make it necessary for us to use diesel power in switching. Notable are the immediate transportation needs for national defense, smoke prevention, and certain situations where coal-burning locomotives are prohibited from entering industries with extreme fire hazards. Even after the new diesel switching locomotives are delivered, coal will still be the fuel for 60 percent of our switching power." It was not necessary to issue further comment on freight power, and for good reason; Paducah Shops were busy at work, rebuilding and refining—perfecting—steam for their freight service. Why, who besides IC would even dream of getting 104,000 pounds of tractive effort out of a 2-10-2!

My closest encounter with IC steam took place one cold February night while visiting my college roommate in Onarga, Ill., over the weekend. He knew my love for railroading and was not the least surprised when I opted for going over to the nearby IC main to watch some trains. At some point on Saturday, a neighbor mentioned a "coal chute being out in a field north of Gilman a little ways." Finding that field north of nearby Gilman quickly, and I guess selfishly, became my immediate objective. The gals we were dating were back on campus, and this Saturday night was one for the railroad! Gilman is only three miles north of Onarga, and that big old coal chute was, indeed, out in the middle of a field north of town. This was as good a time as ever to introduce my roommate to the night world, nay, the *midnight* world of freight trains. Three black-as-the-night diesels heading CS7 south came as the opener and the clattering, rampaging rhythm of steel wheels on the rails, a good beginning. Within a matter of minutes, NC2's chime horn was heard south of town, the growl of its diesel engines accelerating from the speed restriction across the TP&W and Gilman line interlocking. The sealed beam headlight on the head of four hard working geeps lit the tangent rail and 7,000 hp worth of new GP-9s was quickly upon us. NC2's raucous passing only served to further embed the fascinating steel scenario of CS7's southbound passing. Through the inky darkness passed the freezers with fruit, the tank cars with oil, box car after box car, hoppers and gons. Have you ever noticed how each *clackity-clack, clackity-clack* of a fast-moving freight seems to get louder? Sort of hypnotic.

Somehow—and most uncharacteristic of steam—one of IC's big-boilered 4-8-2s had crept in from the north while we were watching NC2's noisy parade of passing cars. Not my way of wanting to introduce the uninitiated to steam, whose entry is usually accompanied by its own thunderous applause. Nevertheless, we were looking at the looming hulk of a Paducah-built 2600 moving up to the coal chute with CB9—all business. No whistle, no bell, no noisy fanfare, just the swirling steamy breath of a hot, clean-fired locomotive. Her cyclops headlight dimmed as she eased to a stop under the chute. She was immense at night! The familiar railroad sounds and smells were comforting. Shadowy black shapes of those who tended her darted through the darkness. At this point, I explained what #2604 was all about to my roommate and made known a deep inner urge that I had always managed to squelch—to get up on the tender of a locomotive at night, lie low, and sneak a ride across a division somewhere. I came awfully close to fulfilling this desire at Gilman that night, and would have, had it not been for—of all things—an understanding fireman! "See the engineer. He might give you a dry ride [in the cab]. He won't take ya both, I know." I pointed up toward the tank and gestured sssshhh with my index finger across my lips. My roommate quickly understood I'd be gone all night. "Go ahead. Hold on and stay low" came the fireman's response. "We'll be out of here before number 17 [*The Night Diamond*]" Up the back of the tender I went.

What followed over the next forty-eight or so miles to Champaign was, perhaps, my favorite experience with steam and one I could easily spend several pages describing: The barking tempo through the big stack into the icy brilliance, moonlight etching our swirling steam; the orange from the fire dancing all around; the engine's shadow on the right-of-way when we passed the lights of a tower. The solid thumping of the 12-wheel tank over crossovers and switches; once underway, passing between silvery grain elevators and through sleeping towns; the most beautiful whistle in the world, warning empty grade crossings of our approach. And once again out in the country, the Heaven full of diamonds, and signals—all green, for miles, like emeralds on black velvet. Yes, Illinois Central will forever be a part of me.

Finally, of all of the colorful paint schemes pictured in this chapter, one must be singled out—the GM&O. Surely top honors for the longest continuously used colors has to go to the Alton and subsequently the Gulf, Mobile & Ohio. The GM&O was formed in 1940 with the merger of the old Gulf, Mobile & Northern and the Mobile & Ohio. At the time, the GM&N was operating its famous little *Rebel* diesel trains, built by ACF in 1935 and painted crimson and silver. Within four years the GM&O became seriously interested in taking over the neighboring Alton Railroad which had been handed over to the bankruptcy court by its owner, the B&O. During the takeover proceedings, the Alton's receivers had purchased new diesels painted in the old predecessor Chicago & Alton colors of red and maroon, which dated back to the famous Alton Limited "red train" of 1899. GM&O's president, Ike Tigrett went on record as "falling in love" with the colors when he saw them and decreed that the GM&O would adopt them. (Although the GM&O/Alton merger did not officially occur until mid 1947, GM&O had been in physical control of the Alton for well over a year with its diesels operating regularly on the Alton.) It should be noted that during the war, a few of the big Alton 5290-series Pacifics received the red and maroon paint, with a huge Alton emblem on the tender. When the GM&O took over, (but well before the actual merger), the emblem was replaced by "the Alton Route" in script on the tender, that slogan being the only road name identification on the locomotives. After the official merger, the GM&O initials were added along the top of the tender sides right under the coal collar, making it official. The red and maroon Pacifics lasted a scant matter of weeks under the GM&O banner as by late 1948, all passenger operations were handled by diesels. In 1949, the entire road dieselized, leading the nation's railroads in dieselization, and leaving steam only a memory. (My only mention of today: as of this writing, there are *still* some red and maroon GM&O F-units in operation!) That's right, 1899.

In 1955 and 1956, Union Pacific and Wabash took delivery of the last brand-new Pullman cars as an era of travel was coming to an end. Just as surely as the diesel locomotive's vastly superior efficiency was vanishing steam, the DC-6s and Connies were placing Pullman cars (let alone whole trains) on the side tracks. And what the airliners couldn't do, the new super highways would. During the march of progress, change is always inevitable. Sails gave way to steam, horses to tractors . . . After the War, stainless steel and vista domes rendered the standard heavyweight passenger train obsolete; well, almost. The Soo Line was a railroad that let the streamliner rush past and seemed content with operating pre-World War I rolling stock—I should say excellent re-conditioned pre-World War I rolling stock—on its overnight *Laker*, between Chicago and Duluth. The wine red train was a perennial favorite for those few who rode its immaculate coaches, the Shoreham Shops rebuilt cafe-lounge cars and the beautiful vintage sleeping cars. And certainly, Soo's dining car boss, Joe Christensen, saw to it that the finest steaks and the heartiest breakfasts be served to the *Laker's* patrons. I, for one, am grateful that the Soo made it possible for us to enjoy the pleasures of yesterday.

This chapter takes us down to St. Louis and over to Kansas City. In an era when the technological changes I mentioned were almost eliminating individuality, mention should be made of Frisco's red and gold racehorse E-8 diesels and the fact that each was given its own name. Names like "Twenty Grand," "Four Deuces," "Gallant Fox," "Big Red" . . . Certainly a fitting way to ease the transition toward conformity.

"All dressed up with nowhere to go." The story was repeated time and time again toward the end of steam—fast, powerful passenger locomotives relegated to protection service, pusher assignments, work train duty, and—in the case of Nickel Plate's fine 90 mph, 74"-drivered 4-6-4 #173—local freight work. She's a beauty to behold . . . but what about that peddler train of hers! The days of varnish are all but memories this summer's eve on the Ft. Wayne Division in September 1957. (WIDELL)

129

For those of us who have spent a good portion of our lives near the East Coast, it is often difficult to associate the New York Central System with Chicago. We tend to forget that New York Central operates 11,000 miles of main line between New York, Boston, Chicago and St. Louis, and we forget the fact that the Central was the first eastern road to enter Chicago. No, New York Central is very much a Chicago railroad, with its two-track main from Buffalo and its two-track Michigan Central coming in from the east. There's a main from Cincinnati and a line from Cairo, Ill., coming to Chicago, too. And one must not forget that the busy Indiana Harbor Belt is a subsidiary of the New York Central. The Central's great steel fleet of streamliners *is* the essence of Central and receives most of the publicity, but it is the freight that brings in over eighty percent of the revenues. On this spread, however, following the general trend, we'll take a look at the twenty percent side of the operating revenues!

The stunning shot above, taken in April 1945, is of brand new Niagara #6000 at the Englewood engine house in Chicago. The glistening 4-8-4 is having her fire cleaned, the hot ash running off the steaming clinkers like lava out of a volcano. #6000 represents the dawn of a new era of locomotive efficiency, power and utilization on the Central, for soon she'll be piling up records with twenty-six sisters that will receive much attention and justifiable praise throughout the industry. At upper right, and to show how quickly the rail industry changed, it's June 12, 1954, and one of the celebrated Niagaras leaves Chicago—not on the *Century,* or on an eighteen-car train, but on the point of train No. 10, a nameless local making all the stops to Buffalo. To add insult to injury, diesels will take over on the short train at Linndale (Cleveland), as Central is 100 percent diesel from there on east. At lower right, on a frozen Feb. 12, 1948, E-7 diesels emerge from a snow squall off the lake into Englewood on the *20th-Century Limited*—OT from New York. (HARLEY, VAN DUSEN, KERRIGAN)

Some vignettes on the two prominent electric railroads serving Chicago—the Chicago, South Shore & South Bend and the Chicago, North Shore & Milwaukee. Above, certainly more reminiscent of main line railroading than an interurban operation is the sight of a 272-ton South Shore "Little Joe" motor rolling merchandise along the well-ballasted main near Michigan City, Ind., in the fall of '57. At upper right, three-cars depart Michigan City for Chicago, while at lower right, two of the road's venerable 900-class freight motors perform switching duties at Michigan City in November 1957. The railroad's home office and shops are located in Michigan City.

The North Shore Line certainly falls into the heavy interurban catagory, while it can be debated whether the South Shore is an electric railroad or interurban. Ironically, the only modern streamliners on either road are North Shore's 90-mph *Electroliners*. At left, the 5:00 *Electroliner* is pictured on its northbound run just east of Ridge Avenue in Evanston in November of '57. The train left Howard Street (Evanston) at 5:29 with its next stop at Kenosha, Wisc., 44 miles and 44 minutes away. This includes two 15 mph restrictions through So. Upton Jct. and No. Chicago Jct., plus 20 mph street-crossing restrictions in Waukeegan! Not bad! (BALL)

Player with Railroads and the
Nation's Freight Handler
            —*Carl Sandburg*

hicago's grip on the railroads can be
lt throughout the midwest as trains
ead in and out of the great center on
ils that radiate in and out of the city
ke spokes from the hub of a giant
heel. In Chicagoland itself, the inner
ythms of the city can be constantly
ard and felt, and they are very much
ilroad. The clack of railroad cars
rrying livestock, the automobile-like
rns on the I.C. electric, the shrill whis-
e from a railroad yard somewhere, the
avy steel trains of the North Shore,
mbling around the Loop's anachron-
tic elevated tracks, the throaty roar
 the *Lake Cities* heading east out of
earborn, behind E-8s. All of this is
nicago—a bustling city of intense vi-
lity.

The trains pictured here are all a part
 Chicago and the midwest. The rail-
ads represented are eastern and
utheastern, but all tie up in the Windy
ty. As we "approach" Chicago in this
ok, we see B&O's *Washington Express*
pper right) at Gary, on Sept. 5, 1953;
&O's big K-2 Mike #1172 (lower right)
riving at Peru, Ind., with No. 90, the
xpediter on Aug. 6, 1950; Erie's Alco-
wered *Flying Saucer* heading west
rough Creston, Ohio (at bottom left)
d, of course, Erie's *Lake Cities* depart-
g Dearborn station for New York bend E-8s on Oct. 14, 1955. (COLLINS, COLLINS,
N DUSEN, VAN DUSEN)

When you take thirty separate railroad companies operating over 4,000 miles of track in and around Chicago and squeeze them all into an area 10 by 20 miles in size, you've got a lot of trains, a lot of color. On these two pages, we're looking at the gamut of diesel road power, from main line passenger types to local commuter and freight engines—a good sampling of the color of Chicago's railroads!

At left, a new Baldwin 48-wheel 6,000 h.p. "centipede" diesel gets a thorough looking over by mechanics at the Pennsy diesel service area at 14th Street, Chicago, on June 21, 1947. The construction is for the new diesel shops. (Do you suppose they don't know how to get her started?) At lower left, a brand new Rock Island EMD FP-7 gets her first workout on a commuter train on Aug. 21, 1949. She's shown at Joliet, Ill. At right, two Chicago & Eastern Illinois F-3s are shown on Oct. 13, 1951, after cutting off their freight. A gyrating warning light was added in the headlight casing, so a new headlight was applied on the center of the nose. Below, the baggage is put aboard and the time 'til departure is only seconds away; on the business end of the *Pere Marquette* is a brand new E-7 diesel from EMD. The Chicago-bound train is pictured on Apr. 3, 1948, at Grand Rapids, Mich., 184 miles from its destination at Grand Central Station (*Left page,* KERRIGAN; *right page,* VAN DUSEN)

We're looking at the diesel that finally broke the back of steam (above), looming high—if not down right imperiously—above the beaten steam in Santa Fe's Corwith yard, Chicago, in April 1941. By year's end 1940, diesels had pushed their radiators, grills, and metal snouts onto the head end of switching chores, commuter runs, and high speed long distance varnish, *but not* onto the head end of redball fast freights. This would remain the domain of big 4-8-4s, 2-10-4s, 4-6-6-4s and the like. In early 1941, this would all change when EMD's new 4,500 h.p. FT diesel freighter #100 entered revenue service for owner Santa Fe. The 193-ft.-long, 428-ton quadruple diesel latched onto

a revenue freight in Los Angeles and headed east, hoping to make it to Chicago. Up the Cajon climb in Run-8 and down the other side on its dynamic brake with the air in release, and across the desert at seventy—bypassing every water plug along the way, #100 ran easily all the way to Chicago! For diesels, the last big frontier had been crossed and a new era begun.

At upper right and taken on the same April day as the shot in Corwith, the *Chief* makes its glorious thunderous departure out of Chicago behind the fiery procession of its 3400-class heavy Pacific and 3461-class Hudson. With diesels now working all types of assignments on the Santa

Fe, you can bet that never again will the wonderous spectacle of working steam be taken for granted. The snorting duo will highball the *Chief* 651.4 miles to Kansas City, where one of the road's enormous 4-8-4s will take over for the grueling 1,788.7-mile run to Los Angeles. At lower right, Santa Fe's pioneer box cabs 1 and 1A growl out of Chicago past 21st Street and I.C.'s high line, heading the outbound *Kansas Cityan*. Like #100, these units made diesel history, though a few years earlier—in 1936—when they made a record-breaking run from Los Angeles to Chicago. By June of '41, when this picture was taken, the two box cabs had been modified with a shovel nose and new front and rear trucks with outside idler axles. By June of '41, these relatively new units were already relics from the incubation years of passenger train diesels, having been superseded by truly streamlined diesels. (HARLEY)

139

America's most colorful railroad competitor were surely the Milwaukee and the Chicago North Western, competing for the lucrative business between Chicago and Milwaukee. (On the longer haul to Minneapolis, the competition was equally fierce between the two roads but with an additional road on this run—the Burlington—to contend with.) On July 15, 1934, both roads agreed to run their trains on a 90-minute schedule over the 85 miles between the two cities, including all stops. On May 29, 1935, the Milwaukee introduced a stunning new 100-mph steam-powered streamlined train, the *Hiawatha*. All of the glamorous century-mark headlines were quickly subdued by the C&NW, however, when a newly re-built, oil-burning class E-2 Pacific hauled conventional equipment between Chicago and Milwaukee at the same record speeds. The gentlemen's agreement remained in effect. In 1939, the C&NW placed four sleek new EMD diesels on the *400* run, amid tremendous fanfare—too much for the Milwaukee! Milwaukee pulled out all the stops and ran a standard Hudson-powered train from Chicago to Milwaukee in an incredible 67½ minutes, breaking all records! Gentlemen's agreements were dumped as the steam vs. diesel vs. steam battle took shape. Now, it would become one of having the best super elevation, the heaviest rail and fewest signals

At left, on Sept. 14, 1948, huge streamlined F-7 Hudson #127 (Baltic #127 to a Milwaukee man!) hits an easy 100 through the Armour estate at West Lake Forest, Ill., heading for Milwaukee. At lower left, on June 8, 1947, rival C&NW's beautiful *Twin Cities 400* nears the Canal Street interlocking in Evanston behind E-6s also heading for Milwaukee. At right, and a little off Milwaukee's beaten path, an A-B-A set of FM diesel-freighters rattles the bolts on the TP&W diamond at Webster, Ill., on May 14, 1954, heading north on the Terre Haute line. The fireman's shouts to the operator are obviously lost in the ruckus! Below, the classic "¾ Lucius Beebe wedge" of Milwaukee's great S-2 class 4-8-4 was made on Oct. 20, 1946, on the Armour estate. The clean-fired Northern is heading its train southbound to the Chicago yards at Bensonville. Beautiful! (*FM diesels,* VAN DUSEN; *all others,* KERRIGAN)

On the preceding page, we looked at the Milwaukee and the Chicago & North Western; now it's time to take another (quick) look at the railroad that grew up with the city of Milwaukee—and stayed, maintaining one of the largest car-building plants in the country, as well as its own West Milwaukee Locomotive Shops.

When *streamline* came into vogue in the mid-30s, the Milwaukee Road launched an aggressive program under its imaginative Chief Mechanical Officer, K. F. Nystrom, to come up with its own high speed, light weight streamliners. Noted industrial designer Otto

Kuhler was retained to design "the very best," no matter what the cost. The most stunning products to emerge from this streamline *Hiawatha* era were the magnificent 84"-drivered F-7 Hudsons, built by American Locomotive Company in 1938 and styled—sheathed—in maroon, black, battleship gray and orange, complemented with chrome ornamental wings and striping. The drama of the *Hiawatha* trains on the 100 mph racetrack comes alive in these two snowy actions at Techny, Ill. On top, an F-7 Hudson whips the *Chippewa Hiawatha* along, while below it, the Otto Kuhler-designed Alco-DL-109 twin unit

#14 slices through the cold air with the *Afternoon Hiawatha*. The 5th car back is coach 477, painted red, white and blue with the patriotic message "Buy War Bonds." #14 was built by Alco in 1941 and represented Milwaukee's first thoughts of dieselization. At right, a brand new Erie-built Fairbanks Morse A-B-A set of diesels is pictured at Minneapolis on June 29, 1947. This Loewy-styled 6,000 h.p. combo was delivered for *Olympian Hiawatha* service and still sported Milwaukee's ornamental chrome—postwar out of the factory! (HARLEY, HARLEY, LAVAKE)

The pictures on this spread were all taken as Chicago & North Western approached its hundredth year of operation; from modest midwest beginnings when predecessor Galena and Chicago Union Railroad started regular service out of Chicago to Maywood, Ill., ten miles, in October 1848. Above, an "Omaha engine," heads a northbound freight through bucolic Tuscobia, Wisc., the fireman obliging with the smoke. The J-A class 2-8-2 was originally built in 1916 for North Western's Chicago, St. Paul, Minneapolis & Omaha Railway. At left, a beautiful shot of a C&NW extra behind F-3s, flying white, sweeping through the curve at Nachusa, Ill., heading west on Aug. 16, 1948. This is the Lee County Cutoff, bypassing Dixon, along with some severe grades on the main line. To the right, from top to bottom: the eastbound *City of Denver* behind units CD 07A, 07B and 5C through Geneva, Ill., on Dec. 26, 1947; the southbound *Peninsula 400* roaring through Rogers Park, Ill., behind North Western's only DL-109, and an EMD mate; and a huge class E-4 Hudson working her heavy train, the eastbound *Pacific Limited* out of the station stop at Geneva, Ill., on Aug. 1, 1948. The big 4-6-4s were used on the Omaha line where their huge 84″ drivers and tremendous tractive effort could be "unleashed" over the flatlands. (*Top left*, PICKETT; *all others*, KERRIGAN)

144

Soo Line, or more formally, the Minneapolis, St. Paul & Sault Ste. Marie, is a granger road that "lives off the land." The annual grain crop contributes to over a third of Soo's traffic. Above, the 75″-drivered #5001 is reflected in a pastoral setting, rushing north along the 452-mile Chicago–Minneapolis run, through Antioch, Ill. At upper right, another summer scene along the Soo, this time with a newer F-7 and F-3 heading out of Shawano, Wisc.

At lower left and lower right, two scenes from nearby Chicago Great Western, itself an agricultural railroad. At left, hotshot second No. 192 changes crews at the road's centralized Oelwein, Iowa, yards (and headquarters)—the power being the usual A-B-B-B-B-A lashup of F-3s andF-7s. Below, one of CGW's thirty-six class T 2-10-4s is pictured on a frosty day in February 1941, heading No. 143 across the big Fox River Bridge at St. Charles, Ill. No one would have guessed that all steam would vanish off the road in less than a decade. (HARLEY, VAUGHN, WALLIN COLLECTION, HARLEY)

Often, one particular class of locomotive is associated with a certain railroad. Certainly such is the case with the Duluth, Missabi & Iron Range and its great 2-8-8-4 Yellowstones. The temptation to throw one or two Yellowstones onto this spread was a great one, but this time I indulged myself with "the other DM&IR." No apologies are in order, believe me. Making up in looks for what it "lacks" in comparative power to a 2-8-8-4 (mind you, I said *comparative* power), the original class E-4 Texas-type #700 is pictured, approaching and passing, throwing her formidable 96,700 pounds of tractive effort onto the rail, working the jennies up Proctor Hill, out of Duluth. #700 and fifteen other beautiful 2-10-4s were procured from sister U.S. Steel railroad, Bessemer & Lake Erie, in 1951, and remained in service on DM&IR's Proctor Hill, and Steelton Hill, as well as on the "cross-country ore run" between Hibbing and Biwabik, right up until the end of steam. Duluth is in the distance and the water, of course, part of Lake Superior. As you can see, the big Texas has been doing a lot of climbing!

Although seemingly out of character with this big ore-hauler, the DM&IR did provide passenger service—usually a two- or three-car spic-and-span train with postal service, baggage and coach. Motive power varied from Pacifics to Mikes. In May 1954, the road ordered Budd self-propelled Rail Diesel Cars (RDCs) in an effort to trim expenses, speed up and modernize the service. By 1961, after pre-viously discontinuing certain passenger runs, the road realized that *no* passenger service could pay for itself, and the last passenger trains came off, ending sixty-seven years of continuous service.   Left, "diesel rail car No. 1," as DM&IR schedules it, prepares to leave Ely for Proctor, over the Iron Range Division. All three photographs were taken on June 16, 1955. (PICKETT)

aseball, apple pie, mother-
ood and Burlington! The
hicago, Burlington &
uincy (known affection-
ely as the "Q") began in
849 as the Aurora Branch
ailroad, operating twelve
iles from the prairie town
f Aurora, Ill., to Turner
unction, connecting with
e new Galena and Chicago
nion Railroad. Service
egan to Chicago in 1850,
nd from these humble be-
innigns, the granger road
as grown to an 11,000-mile
ystem serving fourteen
tates. The Burlington
ioneered the first U.S.
ailway Post Office service,
he diesel streamliner, the
Vista Dome and yes—steam
excursions! The road was
best known for its stainless
steel *Zephyr* streamliners,
including the famed *California Zephyr,* shown later in
this book.

During the fall of '56, long
after many railroads had
gotten rid of their steam
power, a heavy sugar beet
rush and general upturn in
the traffic meant the return
of lovingly-stored steam
power to main line service.
Above left, in October 1956,
one of the Q's handsome M-4
class 2-10-4s marches merchandise through Mendota,
Ill., on a Chicago to Galesburg run. At immediate
left on A-B-B-A quartet of
F-T diesels pilots a
westbound through Gales-
burg the following March,
with plenty of stored steam
in evidence, awaiting their
next call. At far lower right,
M-4 #6323 makes a service
stop in Mendota in October
1956. The 5629—one of Burlington's prized 0-5 class
4-8-4s—is shown in Lincoln,
Neb., during the grain rush
in September 1957. At upper
right, the 1939-era "Silver
Charger" shovel nose diesel
hits a dwindling patch of
sunlight, racing train No.
1—this is train No. 1—a
milk run from West Quincy
to St. Louis in September
1956. This same secondary
train will return as No. 44,
more like a secondary train
number should be! (PICKETT,
BALL, WALLIN, PICKETT, BALL)

For several years, the Illinois Central's fines steam power and newest passenger diesels co-existed on calendars, ticket envelopes, an nual reports, PR brochures, official photos—and on the railroad! It seemed as though the perfect compromise had been reached on the I.C., with the sleek, colorful diesels on the streamliners, and the functional, workaday black steam locomotives o freight.

When I.C. *did* start to bring GP-9 freigh diesel replacements onto the property, man agement saw fit to leave them somber black—apparently out of practicality—but one has to surmise also out of sentiment, as i to cushion the blow!

At upper left, the brand new *City of Miam* barrels down the high-speed main south-bound below Champaign, Ill.; on a beautifu May 16, 1948. To the upper right, as viewec from the city park, 2-10-2 #2701 interrupt the goings-on at Duquoin, Ill., pulling a co train off the secondary line from Benton, Ill to the mainline interchange. At right, one of the road's beautiful Mountain types is ser-viced at Carbondale, between runs on coal. At left, those GP-9s exemplify that "all bus ness" look, backing past I.C.'s finest in stean to assume charge of a main line run to Men phis. The location is Duquoin, and #2604 h been assigned to coal train service. The dat for all of the steam shots is September 1958 and, incredibly, within a year, the "Main Line of Mid-America" would be all diesel!
(KERRIGAN, WALLIN, WALLIN, BALL)

When you've got a good thing going for you, stay with it! I'm talking about the Gulf, Mobile & Ohio's paint scheme, of course, and perhaps America's most colorful railroad. The beautiful maroon, red and gold paint scheme is an historical jewel: It dates back to predecessor Chicago & Alton's famous "red train" the *Alton Limited* of 1899! Through mergers, takeovers and many managements, the red paint survived in one fashion or another, clear through the eventual demise of the GM&O (details in text) At upper left—WOW! We're watching 6,000 h.p. worth of F-3 and F-7s bringing hotshot No. 33 down along 3rd Street in Springfield, Ill., St. Louis-bound from Chicago. Up until now, it was hard to believe that this beautiful September day could be improved! At upper right, and on another beautiful day, GM&O's RS-2 #1513 heads the local freight east through Dwight, Ill., on Aug. 20, 1950. Below, and this could be the rarest shot in the book, GM&O's red, maroon, gold, black and gray Pacific #5296 is shown leaving Brighton, Ill., with the southbound *Alton Limited* in March 1947. #5296 is a class P-167, formerly Alton 656. The elegant 4-6-2's diesel replacements are on the way, but on this first run out of the shop, pride in the railroad couldn't be higher. At lower left, six years later, the maroon and red Pacific is but a dream, as two E-7s chant away, on the point of the southbound *Ann Rutledge* at, appropriately, Lincoln, en route to St. Louis. (WALLIN, BALL, VAN DUSEN, WALLIN COLLECTION)

No doubt about the fact that Missouri Pacific's pastel-colored timetables showing the diesel-powered *Eagle* in a colorful setting "from the mountains to the Missouri" was a strong factor in influencing my boyhood love for the railroad. Seeing the *Eagle* in the flesh, be it from trackside, to the diner (with its pastel *Eagle* dinnerware), or sneaking into the parlor observation to watch the speedometer, was always a special experience. (Why there were even small illuminated ornamental Christmas trees at each table in the diner and parlor at Christmas time!)

At right, May 1954, two FA-powered freights are ready to head east out of Jefferson City, Mo., to St. Louis. That's the majestic state capitol in the background. Far right, the streamlined *Missouri River Eagle* makes its two-minute crew change, mail and passenger stop, en route to Kansas City and Omaha. The beautiful train carries a planetarium dome, club car, diner-bar-lounge, coaches and sleepers. Below, the Raymond Loewy-designed parlor observation, with its full relief aluminum Eagle, brings up the rear of the departing train. When originally delivered by ACF in 1939, the *Eagle* equipment's unique exterior aluminum trim matched, from diesel to obs. Bottom right, Sedalia Shop's 75″-drivered super dual-service Northern brings an eastbound freight into Kirkwood, Mo., in the summer of 1950. (#2113-R. W. GISH, WALLIN COLLECTION; ALL OTHERS, BALL)

Where did you see your first diesel passenger train? What railroad? And which train? Depending on what part of the country you were in, and whether or not you were more or less on the "ground floor" of dieselization, chances are you were enraptured by the diesel's rainbow colors, elegance, power—and yes, excitement. If you were lucky enough to be near more than one railroad, then the first impressions inevitably led to comparisons, and ultimately, "favorites" among the new-hued diesels. Some of the colorful trains that come up from the south and southwest into Kansas City and St. Louis are pictured on this spread. Each of these trains was a favorite (but then, what train wasn't?!). Above, Kansas City Southern's fast-moving *Southern Belle* roars over the U.S. 71 Highway overpass in Grandview on the edge of town, minutes from its appointed 10:00 A.M. arrival at Kansas City's Union Station on Dec. 23, 1953. At immediate right, the two million dollar joint Frisco-MKT premier train, the *Texas Special*, arrives at St. Louis on its run from San Antonio, Ft. Worth, and Dallas. At upper left, Frisco's standard-equipped train No. 112, the *Oklahoman*, drawn by an E-8 named after race horse Gallant Fox makes a mail stop at Hillsdale, Kansas, on Apr. 20, 1954, running late on its twelve-hour, 379-mile stop-or-be-flagged-everywhere run from Oklahoma City. At left, an unexpected treat in the summer of '52 as Katy's northbound *Bluebonnet* appeared just south of Merriam, Kansas, behind a trim 73″-drivered Pacific, pinch-hitting for the usual PA diesels. Even though the 4-6-2 had been relegated to "protection power status," its appearance still conveyed the *true color* of railroading. (BALL, BALL, BALL, COLLECTION)

Rock Island's pioneer TA diesel #606 is serviced at Memphis
in July 1952, along with a mate. On Sept. 19, 1937, sister
#601, the first of six of the little 1,200 h.p. diesels, inaugu-
rated the new streamlined four-car *Peoria Rocket* from Peoria
to Chicago and return, commencing a new era of streamlined
Rockets that would eventually service—and change—the entire railroad. (LAVAKE)

160

5

DISTANT HORIZONS

ATCHISON, TOPEKA AND SANTA FE RAILWAY CO.
CHICAGO, BURLINGTON & QUINCY RAILROAD
CHICAGO, MILWAUKEE, ST. PAUL AND PACIFIC RAILROAD
CHICAGO, ROCK ISLAND AND PACIFIC RAILROAD CO.
COLORADO AND SOUTHERN RAILWAY CO.
DENVER & RIO GRANDE WESTERN RAILROAD CO.
GREAT NORTHERN RAILWAY
KANSAS CITY SOUTHERN LINES
NATIONAL RAILWAYS OF MEXICO
NORTHERN PACIFIC RAILWAY
ST. LOUIS-SAN FRANCISCO RAILWAY CO.
ST. LOUIS SOUTHWESTERN RAILWAY LINES
SOUTHERN PACIFIC LINES
TEXAS AND PACIFIC RAILWAY CO.
UNION PACIFIC RAILROAD

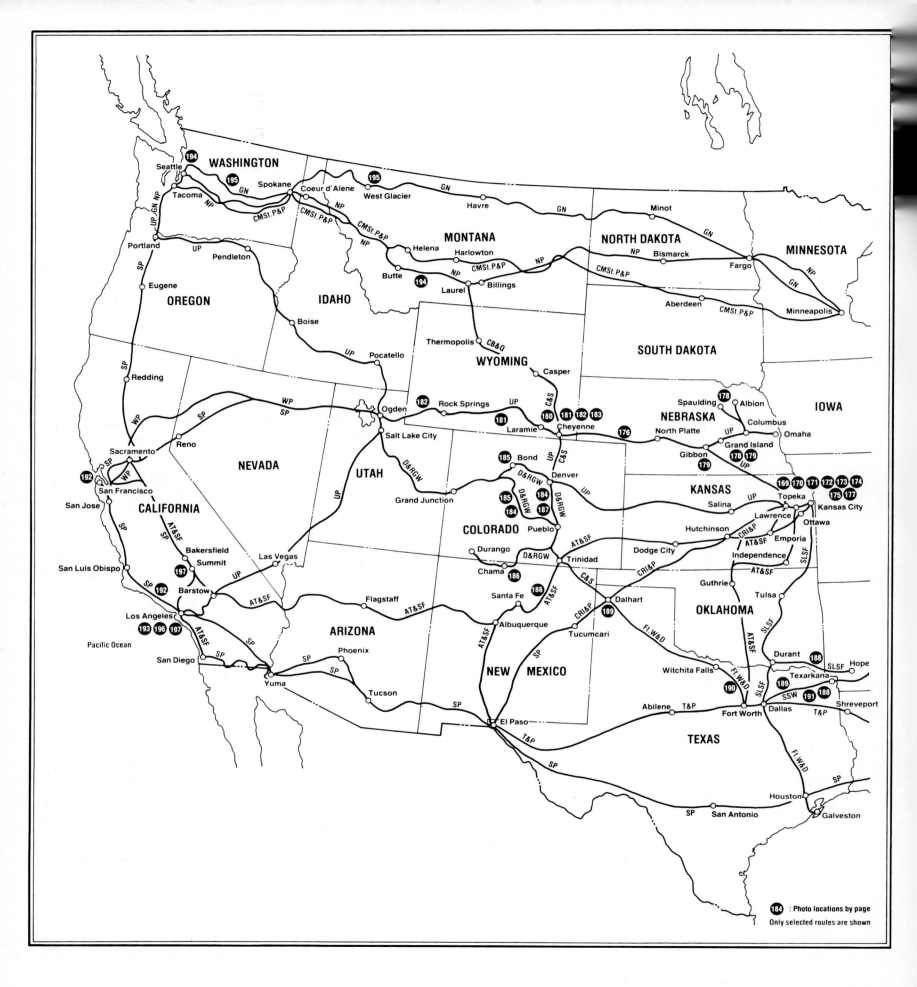

WASHINGTON
Seattle 194
195 Spokane
Tacoma
NP
GN
UP-GN-NP
Portland
UP
Pendleton
SP
Eugene
OREGON

Coeur d'Alene
195 West Glacier
CMSt.P&P
CMSt.P&P
NP
CMSt.P&P
NP
IDAHO
Boise
UP
Pocatello

MONTANA
Helena
Harlowton
Butte
194 Laurel Billings
CMSt.P&P NP
NP

Havre
GN

NORTH DAKOTA
NP Bismarck
CMSt.P&P Aberdeen

Minot
GN
GN
Fargo
CMSt.P&P
NP
GN
Minneapolis
MINNESOTA

Thermopolis
CB&Q
WYOMING
Casper

SOUTH DAKOTA

IOWA

WP
SP
Redding

Reno
Sacramento
SP
192
San Francisco
WP
San Jose
CALIFORNIA

Ogden
182 Rock Springs UP
181
Salt Lake City
C&S
180 181 182 183
Laramie Cheyenne
176
UP C&S

NEVADA
UTAH
D&RGW
UP
Grand Junction
185 Bond
D&RGW
185 184
D&RGW
184 187 Denver
COLORADO
Pueblo

Spaulding 178 Albion
Columbus
NEBRASKA
North Platte
UP Omaha
Grand Island
178 179
Gibbon 179
UP

169 170 171 172 173 174
175 177
Topeka
KANSAS Kansas City
Salina UP
Lawrence
Ottawa
Hutchinson CRI&P
AT&SF Emporia
Independence SLSF

San Luis Obispo
SP
192
Bakersfield
197 Summit
Barstow
AT&SF
Los Angeles
193 196 197
SP
AT&SF
Pacific Ocean
San Diego
SP
Yuma

Las Vegas
UP
Flagstaff
AT&SF
ARIZONA
SP
Phoenix
SP
Tucson
SP

Durango
D&RGW
Chama 186
Santa Fe 186
AT&SF
Albuquerque
AT&SF
NEW MEXICO
SP
El Paso
T&P

Trinidad
Dodge City
CRI&P
C&S
CRI&P
Dalhart
189
Ft.W&D
Tucumcari
CRI&P

Guthrie
OKLAHOMA
AT&SF
Tulsa
SLSF

Witchita Falls
Ft.W&D
190
Abilene
T&P
Fort Worth
SLSF
Durant 188
SLSF Hope
Texarkana
189
SSW 191 188
Dallas Shreveport
T&P
TEXAS
Ft.W&D
SP
Houston
SP San Antonio
Galveston

184 : Photo locations by page
Only selected routes are shown

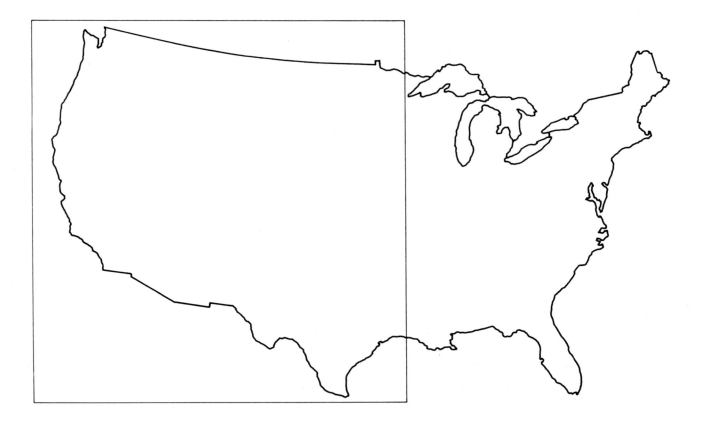

169 Bonner Springs, Ks.

170 Turner, Ks.

171 Loring, Ks.

172 Zarah, Ks.

170, 172–73 Holliday, Ks.

177 Menoken, Ks.

176 Ogalalla, Neb.

178 Spalding, Neb.

179 Gibbon, Neb.

178–79 Grand Island, Neb.

180–83 Sherman Hill

182 Green River, Wyo.

181 Rawlins, Wyo.

184 Tennessee Pass

184, 187 Colorado Springs, Colo.

185 Minturn, Colo.

186 Wagon Mound, N.M.

189 Dalhart, Tex.

188 Idabel, Okla.

189 Ridgeway, Tex.

190 Decatur, Tex.

191 Mineola, Tex.

191 Mt. Pleasant, Tex.

192 Chatsworth, Cal.

194 Livingston, Mont.

194 Seattle, Wash.

195 Glacier Park, Mont.

195 Wenatchee, Wash.

197 Cajon Pass

IN THE EARLY 1800s several enterprising pioneers started a small settlement near the Missouri River. They envisioned the little settlement ultimately becoming the last trading post and recognized "port of entry" for westward bound settlers. One of the earliest settlers at the outpost was the Rev. Isaac McCoy who established a Baptist mission in 1831. His brother, John, built the area's first general store the following year. "West Port" became the unofficial name for the settlement, and it soon, indeed, became the last inhabited area for westbound wagon trains before they hit the westward trails. Wagon trains heading west made West Port the assembling place for travelers who would then join wagons for the otherwise lonely, difficult and even more dangerous crossing over the Santa Fe, California and Oregon Trails.

West Port would quickly get to know the famed Conestoga wagon, the prairie schooner and the later heavy freight wagons drawn by teams of horses or mules. Blacksmiths were available for iron work and nail making, and wheelwrights were available for any type of repair, be it working new white oak for frames, floor beams, wheel spokes and felloes or hickory for new (or stronger) tongues and shafts, axletrees, bows and singletrees. Yellow poplar was available for side stringers, floorboards and ends, and gum wood for hubs and other small parts. In short, West Port was the last outpost where wagon trains could be checked and outfitted for what lay ahead.

In 1857, the booming settlement could boast having over 5,000 residents, and it was decided to incorporate the outpost into a town to be officially named "Westport." The Civil War soon spread as far as Westport. Its citizens found themselves split down the middle, between Southern sympathizers and the North. A major battle broke out at Westport, and the Union troops took control of the town. The few wagon trains that were moving west now *avoided* Westport. Nearby, another outpost had begun to grow, and soon this nearby center became the burgeoning incorporated city of Kansas, Mo., which become, in time, Kansas City. By 1897, Kansas City annexed Westport in its continuing sprawl. The railroad came to Kansas City in the 1860s. Colonel Holliday's Santa Fe held its auspicious commencement in Kansas City with an earth-turning ceremony on October 30, 1868. Today the greater KC region has sixteen major rail lines.

In the spring of 1954, I had a full two weeks of spring vacation; I was going to squeeze every steam locomotive and railroad I possibly could into every day of that vacation. I would ultimately end up in Lawrence for a quick visit with my grandparents—and a slightly longer visit with the Union Pacific! The Union Pacific offered the only main line steam assignments out of Kansas City. Why just last summer, the Kansas City Southern and the Milwaukee had steam in transfer service; the Santa Fe was a hot-bed of steam-powered trains. Burlington was running some steam, and, of course, Union Pacific was about as solid a steam operation as one could ask for (not counting the long-haul streamliners). Now it was 1954, and I had to change my thinking on the railroad scene. Now I was lucky just knowing that steam was still assigned to trains 39 and 40 between KC and Salina. Let me go back over this one more time, in another light: Last summer I could shoot Union Pacific steam to my heart's content—black and white one day, 16mm color movies the next, and if I wanted, slides the next time, and repeat the process. If it was cloudy or rainy, why I'd wait until I had good sun. The major impediment was lack of funds. Simple. Now it's one year later—really nine months later—and I'd have my crack at two trains behind steam, sun or clouds, good location or bad, two trains, that's it. The dilemma becomes further complicated when I add the fact that the two trains I'm talking about—Nos. 39 and 40—were always my transportation to and from Bonner Springs, where I loved spending the greater portion of a day on the slight grade out of town, where I felt the photographic possibilities were infinately better from the standpoint of surrounding scenery. One half mile west of the depot, the railroad crossed the Santa Fe, and all trains were restricted to 30 mph. I could always be assured that any westbound freight would be working hard a mile west of the crossing, getting underway through Loring. My choice boiled down to one of catching No. 40 at, or arriving in, Lawrence and then riding over to Bonner, or grabbing that arrival shot and then, in hopes of catching one more shot, hightailing it over up-and-down Kansas Rt. 32 toward Bonner Springs in Grandad's Chevy—something I did not want to do.

I did try a race with No. 40 that day, but the aged Chevy Six, backroads, and my less-than-enthusiastic driving proved no match for 3222's 77″ drivers and "permitted speed" of 75 miles an hour. This was the first time in my life I literally had to *run* to catch (or try to catch) a picture of a steam locomotive, and I did not like it. This was a dramatic turning point in my life-long love for trains, as I realized for the first time, *I* would be the one on the run, trying to keep ahead of the diesel. I had to make a grave compromise that day, and for the first time I had to compromise between riding behind steam (to photograph diesels), or photographing steam in one location where I knew I could get it. I couldn't have imagined, in my craziest of dreams that day, what physical, financial and time-consuming hardships lay ahead of me in my drive to keep up with steam—anywhere—as long as it existed. Had I had the slightest inkling of what was ahead, I might have taken up another hobby (and up until that May 1954 day, I had never looked upon my love for trains as a "hobby").

I did drive around Bonner, Loring and Linwood that day, but I was in deep frustration, turmoil. The late spring buds were still bursting—buds on trees that lay dormant all winter long—moths were emerging from cocoons, and ants were building earthly empires all over again. A redwing blackbird called from last autumn's tattered cattail, and blades of grain already were reaching for the sun. It was a lovely time of year—a time of awakening. Spring is always a road of rediscovery, for spring has been here before. If we missed it in other years, it was because we let the season pass by us. Spring is for those who go in search of it. Spring is available to those who know it intimately. Somehow, I wanted to draw a parallel between steam and spring, but I couldn't. I realized that once seen, the beauty of spring could never be taken away.

The old familiar train that I would wait around for and shoot on its late afternoon westward trek was No. 39, of course, a bread-and-butter train that simply went by a number in the timetable. But folks along the line still called it the "City of Salina." This rather strange carryover of tradition, or habit, has deep roots, and when you consider its origin, it makes plenty of good old fashioned horse sense! Back in January 1935, the nation's first streamlined passenger train, the *City of Salina,* was introduced into regular service on precisely the same route. The pioneer three-car yellow and brown streamliner was built by Pullman out of lightweight aluminum alloy and was powered by a 600 h.p. Winton distillate-burning engine. The little train was officially the "M-10000" on the roster, but the Union Pacific's bright-thinking PR people dubbed it "Tomorrow's Train Today." The railroad further saw to it that the *City of Salina* toured the country on a sixty-eight-stop, 13,000-mile stint, which began on February 15, 1934. The *City of Salina* made headlines and became the symbol of the new streamline era. From this humble beginning, the mighty Union Pacific expanded its great fleet of "cities" streamliners to a system-wide fleet. Now, in 1954, I was waiting for train No. 39, the old "City of Salina," because it was an unlike-the-cities local, still drawn by steam.

The following day I took No. 40 into Kansas City and walked out to the Armstrong yards. There I found two rows of recently run but now carefully boarded up 4-12-2s. Their bells, whistles and marker lights were wrapped in cloth and their stacks capped. My personal favorite, #9043, led the stalled parade. I was told they would all be used in the grain rush. Inside the house, the only sign of life was a 2-10-2 under steam (I believe #5052) simmering away under the guise of "protection power." I did not like what I saw but took consolation in the fact that the Nines were freshly painted, lubed—and *100 percent intact*. The highlight of the day was the ride in the cab of #3222, scampering back to Lawrence.

Union Pacific was a heartbreaker in the spring of 1954; but come the next few years, with the help of those three ingredients—physical, financial and time-consuming hardships—*plus* a pass from my summer job with Santa Fe's Engineering Department at Ft. Madison, Iowa, the Union Pacific would again be a major part of my railroad world, though never again through Lawrence.

Two months after this dismal spring vacation, *Trains* Magazine arrived in the mail with a "Steam Power Guide," listing the railroads and location where steam still operated, along with anticipated "D-dates" for the various railroads planning imminent dieselization. "Where steam *still* operated. . . ." I really did not have the heart (or stomach) to come to grips with reality—the fact that a desperate race in my life had begun.

No other railroad in the U.S. (probably anywhere) is more affected by seasonal rushes than the Union Pacific. Burlington has its sugar beets and Santa Fe its potatoes, but Union Pacific has one great big seasonal rush with green fruit, wheat and sugar beets that tops everything! While I was lamenting over dead engines and the general state of affairs on the Kansas Division, I did not know that even then, scores and scores of steam locomotives were stored serviceable in row after row after row at big UP terminals all across Nebraska and Wyoming; and I did not know that in addition to the carefully planned seasonal steam-onslaught, regular assignments were drawing steam year 'round across the Nebraska and Wyoming divisions. Routine work, just the way the Kansas Division was up until this year. For the time being, Union Pacific was yellow diesels, trains 39 and 40, and the little old 2-8-0 #492, which was still in Lawrence to handle the Leavenworth local—on borrowed time.

Omaha, Valley, Grand Island, Kearney, Ogallala, Julesburg, and all points between, would become new haunts across Nebraska, and every bend and bridge on Highway 30 would soon become familiar. "Everything's up on the Nebraska Division" proclaimed the agent at Lawrence. Second only to the Hotel Roanoke for favorite sleeping spots would become the Erin Swiss Motel in Fremont, Nebr. Mr. Murphy would soon know to give me a room in his motor court facing the tracks, one block away from Union Pacific's all-night-long whistle-screaming thunderous parading main line! Steam operation in the late summer of 1955 was pretty much railroading as usual, but in 1956, things began to change, even on the Nebraska Division. In 1956, it looked like the Nines were gone. The operator at Columbus made some inquiries and could have sworn to the fact he had recently seen some, but a check of block sheets for the past two months didn't reveal a single 9000. More investigation revealed that in February, the extra 9007 West, coupled with the extra 9040 West were dispatched light out of Omaha for Grand Island. Did that mean they'd be used in the rush west of Grand Island? In 1957, noticeably absent from the ranks were more favorites—the Harriman 4-8-2s and most of the 2-10-2s. Things had deteriorated to the point where individual engine numbers could be singled out as *survivors*. "The 5040 is still used on the hill out of Council Bluffs. . . ." The old familiar 800 class 4-8-4s and the not-so-familiar 3800 series 4-6-6-4s were pretty much in charge now and were putting on a hell of a show, nudging the markers on many a diesel-powered hotshot. Operating men were especially delighted in the way the big 77"- and 80"-drivered Northerns could wheel the reefers. ("Surprised" is more like it!) Passenger extras were routinely handled by 800s on the fastest time cards on the system, and dispatchers were hard-pressed to get the 800s out ahead of everything else, in order not to put them behind a slower 65 or 70 mph job somewhere! If you were just looking for a steam show—and not for long lost friends from other years—UP's summer show beat 'em all.

The gas turbines ("big blows") were coming onto the railroad in ever-increasing numbers, and they had a nasty habit of throwing up smoke on the distant horizon, looking for all the world like an oil-burning steamer. More than once we were fooled, scrambling to trackside on the double, cameras flailing, only to see the now visible yellow nose. Quite a blow (and lousy pun)! In 1959, several huge 3700 series Challengers wheeled main line assignments between North Platte and Cheyenne. This encore was beautiful but lasted for a scant thirteen days, before the steel strike messed things up. And if you were lucky enough to be standing at trackside west of Cheyenne, you would have witnessed the mightiest-in-the-world Big Boys going forth loudly, proclaiming their great power and domain, as if they'd go on forever. Big Boy was an awesome orator, but this was 1959—the moment when time and eternity would finally intersect.

Union Pacific. I always wondered why Union Pacific was not my absolute favorite railroad. Certainly no other railroad was made up of the romance and history that made up Union Pacific. I'm talking about ten thousand men starting to build the railroad westward out of the river town of Omaha in 1865. This was the Nebraska Territory then, and as one historical account put it, "on the raw edge of civilization." The surveyors started the route west; behind them followed the graders, cutting through the hills, filling in the valleys. Tunnels were blasted and bridges were built. Westward, ever westward. Shovel and pick and black gunpowder were the tools; mules and carts provided the hauling. Behind the graders came the track-layers. Everything was brought into Omaha by steamboat or wagon, from food and ammo to ties, spikes and iron rails. General Jack Casement from the Union Army was the tough boss of the construction crews, and he pushed the men hard. Gamblers and "hangers on" were dealt with the way the red man was. Henry Stanley, a British journalist, braved the cross-country trip to take a first hand look at the construction crews pushing westward and penned: "Soldiers, herdsmen, teamsters, women, railroad men are dancing, singing or gambling. There are men here who would murder a fellow creature for five dollars . . . mostly everyone seems bent on debauchery and dissipation." General Casement organized his men with military precision and never gave up the battle for discipline. He even referred to his westernmost rails as "the front."

And now, ninety years later, here we are on Highway 30—the famed Platte River Road, the route of the Oregon Trail and the Pony Express. The Morman push carts came this way, and so did the forty-niners. The Overland Stage came through here, too. And now, less than ninety years later, it is still possible to picture our forefathers crossing this land, the predecessors of the mighty Union Pacific. All of this studied history was contemplated one day in 1956 at the mouth of the great steel bridge at Omaha that carries the trains out of Council Bluffs across the Missouri River and onto the rails that climb a 1.3 percent grade, twenty-one miles to Lane. Almost in a daze, I watched the great 4-8-4s, 2-10-2s and 4-6-6-4s storm up the tracks, through the spans, past me, disappearing beyond the station and the 7th Street yard. The full implication of what was happening hadn't really hit; I was watching for the 2860, the 3222, the 7004, the 9043, the 9085 . . . I hadn't yet realized they had gone the way of the push carts, the forty-niners, the Overland Stage. . . .

For years, the official slogan for Colorado was "Colorful Colorado." It appeared on license plates, state maps and travel brochures, to name but a few items. Of course, color and scenery are at once synonymous, and I believe very little in the world can compare with the colorful scenery in Colorado. Over the years, I've saved a post card from a family trip to Colorado in 1947, showing the broad face of Pikes Peak taken from the east with the Denver & Rio Grande Western's main in the foreground near, I suppose, Husted, Colo. The all-too-inspiring caption simply says "Colorful Colorado—where vistas stretch the eyes, enlighten the heart, and make the spirit humble." It might be equally cornball to lead into the spreads of Colorado that follow, but what other state offers the color of railroading that Colorado does? And here we can draw the parallel of railroad variety and color to natural scenery and color. I mean where else can you see double-slotted Northerns at work, narrow gauge from the gold and silver days, two-of-a-kind cab unit/booster unit main line diesels, 2-8-8-2s on the rear of coal—Pocahontas coal-road style—and fluted stainless steel diesels with matching passenger equipment . . . *all in one state*. I think our brief look at Colorado railroading is a good one.

I do want to mention those "quick change artist" diesels I refer to briefly in one of the Colorado captions. I'm talking about Rock Island's two special cab-booster units #750 and #751 which were outshopped by EMD in May 1940, for the *Rocky Mountain Rocket*. Every day this dazzling train departs Chicago for Colorful Colorado, terminating in Denver and Colorado Springs. Wait a minute! Denver and Colorado Springs are not on the same line, nor are they remotely convienient to each other. That's right, and that is why the Rock Island ordered two customized B units with head end controls, a 1,000 h.p. engine and baggage compartment. Out of Chicago, on the usually heavy *Rocket,* the 1,000 horses are sandwiched between two ranting 2000 h.p. sisters all the way to Limon, Colo. It is here that the B unit is cut out, and it makes the separate trip to Colorado Springs with three or four cars from the train; the rest of the shebang continuing on to Denver. On the return run, just reverse the process, everyone joining up at Limon for the trip back to Chicago. Ingenious!

In concluding this look at America's colorful railroads, I have to say that surely the Southern Pacific is in top contention for being the most colorful. You can argue on that one. (Certainly many would argue that Texas & Pacific's streamlined *Eagle* passenger trains and freight diesels are as dashing in this age of color as the brass-cap-stacked predecessors that hauled the *Sunshine Special;* but weren't Cotton Belt's diesels America's most colorful?)   I never saw an orange, red, black, white-trimmed GS-4 dashing along the California coast with its matching *Daylight;* I was two years too late. If I had, I'm sure I would go along, hands down, with the widely-held opinion that Espee's passenger trains were the prettiest in the U.S.—or anywhere, for that matter. I'll have to let the pictures speak for themselves.

In my other books, I have singled out two locomotives and two trains that were absolute favorites in my childhood, the locomotives being Union Pacific's heavy 4-6-2 #3222, customarily assigned to the *Kansan,* and Santa Fe's beautiful slant-nosed E-6s customarily on the *Kansas Cityan.* Being a "back light nut," I gladly take this opportunity to show both trains and both locomotives once again. Sad to say, the 3222 is pictured on her last run, Dec. 11, 1954, near Bonner Springs, Kansas. The *Kansas Cityan* is shown ten days later, leaving Kansas City for Lawrence and beyond. To this day, I cannot imagine a nicer looking steam-powered passenger train anywhere! And like the 3222, my commentary on Santa Fe's classy E-6 is that they were the most dashing diesels ever painted up at La Grange! (BALL)

Lucius Beebe, in none too few words said, "N[o] railroad terminal in the American record ev[er] saw the recurrent arrival and departure of such a rich multiplicity of eye-filling name trains under the corporate banners of so ma[ny] carriers over so long a period of time as the [] Union Station in St. Louis." He's probably right, but I'll certainly add that Kansas City cannot be too far behind St. Louis! And whe[n] you add the transcontinental mains of the UP[,] Rock Island and Santa Fe, plus such colorfu[l] roads as the Chicago Great Western, Milwaukee and Kansas City Southern, I'd nominate KC for being *the* center for, and of, America's most colorful railroads—freight an[d] passenger, steam and diesel.

At left, and rolling down a slight sag unde[r] its canopy of oil smoke is one of Santa Fe's beautifully proportioned 2-10-2s heading an extra west through Holliday, Kansas, in January 1952. At lower left, the eastbound Chief glides along the Kaw River east of Turner, Kansas, eight miles out of Kansas City Union Station on Mar. 15, 1959. At upper right, the head brakeman "rides the irons" on the head end of four Kansas City Southern F-7s down past West Wye Tower to Air Line Jct. and waiting manifest freight No. 41— destination Deramus Yard, Shreveport. At lower right, the big Sweeny stacked 3222 talks it up, leading Union Pacific's train No. 39 through Loring, Kansas, on Apr. 23, 1954, nineteen miles from its stop at Lawrence. The Kansas Division local will continue on to Salina. (BALL, BALL, COLLECTION, BALL)

Have you stood along the Santa Fe tracks west of Kansas City? Where the land flattens out and the trains really roll? If you're going to watch the Santa Fe—and get to know her—I'd suggest Kansas as a good place to start.

It was in Kansas that the Santa Fe Trail and the Oregon Trail made their junction; it was in Kansas that the Pony Express route, the Osage Trail, Pike's Route to Pawnee Village, Holladay's Overland Line, the Santa Fe Cutoff and Butterfield's Overland Dispatch Line all crossed and crisscrossed, to say nothing of the Texas cattle trails. It was in Kansas, in Topeka on October 30, 1868, that Colonel Holliday turned the first shovelful of earth and said his new railroad would reach the Gulf of Mexico and out to the Pacific.

Out across Kansas, the ghosts of the sodbusters and the trackspikers and muleskinners are at trackside watching the thunderous passing of the Santa Fe, heading west, over land once accustomed to the thunder of the buffalo and the race of the antelope. It is at the start of the great Osage Plains that we too witness the great trains on the Santa Fe iron trail. Above left, and one of the most classic action shots in this book, Santa Fe's huge Northern #2906 pounds westbound through Zarah, Kansas, on Nov. 27, 1946. This great engine will be on the run all the way from Argentine yard (Kansas City) to Clovis, N.M.—637 miles! At lower left, Santa Fe's heavy Pacific #3440 burnishes the rails through Holliday, Kansas, on the same November day with the westbound *California Limited*. Above, an E-6, the 1A and an E-6B are on the job handling westbound train No. 11, the *Kansas Cityan* through Holliday on Nov. 27, near the point where the Lawrence line cuts off the main line. The three unit combo pictured is the standard lashup on trains 11 and 12. (KERRIGAN)

Some of my favorite trains and locomotives are pictured on this spread—all regulars through Lawrence. At upper right, Santa Fe's train No. 3, the westbound *California Limited* has made its 8:51 A.M. stop and is seen leaving town on Apr. 24, 1954. The bridge in the background leads across the Kaw River to, among other places, the UP depot. The large building is the Jenny Wren flour mill. At lower right, Third 357 does not have a train today, rather a power move/caboose hop following Second 359 on Christmas Day 1953. At upper left, "my engine" #3222 takes time out for water and its station stop at Lawrence, en route west with Union Pacific's train No. 39. Nos. 39 and 40 operated daily between Kansas City and Salina and always drew steam. When a 4-8-4 or a 4-8-2 was not on the head end, you could always count on one of three classy Harriman Pacifics assigned to the Kansas Division, and such was the case on Apr. 24, 1954. At immediate left, Rock Island's *Texas Rocket* makes a flag stop at Lawrence for passengers going to Wichita and beyond. The Rock Island uses the tracks of the UP through Lawrence and is more or less the "orphan" when it comes to passenger train service. (BALL)

The Union Pacific's Nebraska Division and Kansas Division are similar in many ways. The country looks essentially the same, the trains very much alike. Even the history and construction of the two rail lines (the old Kansas Pacific and the UP main) are remarkably similar. The main difference is the fact that the Nebraska Division *is* the Union Pacific main line, while the almost-as-busy Kansas Division is a single-track railroad west of Topeka and a double-track road east of Topeka. To me, what made the Kansas Division different was the fact that the Kansas Division had its own main line local passenger trains, quite unlike the great fleet of transcontinentals that plied the Nebraska line.

The 4,500 h.p. "veranda" gas turbine, pictured above, was built by GE in 1954 and rep-

resents the newest type of motive power in this book. It also represents Union Pacific's "think big" approach to motive power design. No. 63 is shown bypassing the huge coal chute at Ogallala, Neb., speeding empty reefers and grain boxcars westward in August 1959. The fuel oil tender was made from the existing frame and wheel sets off one of the 18,000-gallon tenders from a 4-12-2, and by splicing the water compartments from two of the tenders back to back. This gave the turbine a sizable 24,000-gallon insulated auxiliary fuel tank—enough to get the "big blow" easily over the 992 miles of track from Council Bluffs (Omaha) to Ogden, Utah, without refueling. The turbines, as a rule, did not come down on the Kansas Division, except on occasional crew familiarization runs.

While the first turbines were running across Nebraska in regular service, the standard Kansas Division freight power was the 4-12-2 and 2-10-2, both pictured at right. #9083 is westbound out of Kansas City, heading toward Lawrence on Aug. 30, 1953, with a "cutoff freight" that will take the 251.8-mile Gibbon Cutoff from just west of Topeka, at Menoken, up to Gibbon, Neb., on the Nebraska Division main line. By taking the cutoff, the UP saves a full day getting freight out to the west coast! #5055 is also out of Kansas City, heading west, but is continuing straight across the Kansas Division, bound for Denver. She is also pictured on Aug. 30, 1953, a few miles west of Menoken. (WALLIN, BALL, BALL)

In the old days, what ran Nebraska was the railways, particularly the Union Pacific. The railroads got the land, built on it, developed it, populated it, and then exploited it as they saw fit. At one time, the Union Pacific and Burlington each selected their own state Senator in Nebraska! The power symbol of the railroad continues in Nebraska with the big Union Pacific seemingly everywhere, be it branch or main line. The historically tough image of the railroad remains in lore. One of the railroad stories that started around Omaha during the Second World War was that then Union Pacific President William Martin Jeffers was so tough that he broke half dollars with his teeth!

At top left, in the grain rush of 1957, big power in the form of an 80″-drivered Northern and a 3800-series 4-6-6-4 Challenger back down to their waiting freight trains on the east end of the Grand Island yard. At upper right, #804 has her train underway and is now Extra 804 East on the main, headed toward Omaha . . . headed for some mighty hot running! The 3818 will follow X804's markers out of town as Extra 3818 East, but her 69″ drivers will "restrict" running speed to a somewhat slower 70 mph! Below right, the setting sun catches two FA-powered freights westbound out of Gibbon in August 1959. At lower left, in September 1956, a smoky portrait of the Columbus-Spaulding mixed up on the Cedar Rapids Branch. The little 2-8-0s were as common on the branch lines as grain elevators and cattle pens. (WIDELL, BALL, WIDELL, WALLIN)

The Nebraska Divsion of the Union Pacific follows the valley of the Platte clear across the state, and during the age of steam, the haze of smoke over the constant parade of trains could be seen from Omaha to Cheyenne. From the vast plains to the uplands and finally the mountains, the going gets rougher and the conquering power tougher as you proceed west along UP's iron trail. West of Cheyenne on the Wyoming Division, one quickly realizes how *big* the UP really is, and what it takes to come to grips with—and master—Mother Nature. It is no wonder that the biggest steam locomotives in the world called "Chian" their home. Cheyenne was truly America's Temple of Steam, for nowhere else in the railroad world was big bigger.

At immediate right, a sample of the world's largest. Big Boy #4002 storms westbound out of Cheyenne to conquer Sherman Hill in March 1955. Below, Big Boy #4019 comes in off the "new line" on No. 3 track and joins the old main at Dale. That's the westbound *City of Los Angeles* heading past on track No. 1, five hours behind schedule. The Milwaukee power is in pool service on the "cities streamliners" which travel to Chicago over Milwaukee rails east of Omaha. At upper right, Challenger #3933 drifts downgrade eastbound through Buford, early on December 7, 1941. The crew will hear the news of Pearl Harbor upon arrival in Cheyenne. Below right, a backlit view of the original 4-8-8-4, Big Boy #4000 heading east out of Rawlins in September 1954. "By the time her caboose came, it was dark!" (DONAHUE, WALLIN, KERRIGAN, KERRIGAN)

God give me mountains,
with hills at their knees

—Leigh B. Hanes

Wyoming. Here is America—high, naked, and exposed. Here is unspoiled America, resting a mile high. Wyoming covers almost 100,000 square miles with a population only one-tenth that of Brooklyn. Here is an America where one can still drive for fifty miles and not see a soul! Wyoming has been called "a child of transcontinental trails" as five trails—the Oregon, Overland, Mormon, Bridger and Bozeman—crisscrossed Wyoming. The Pony Express crossed Wyoming, and so did the cattle highway, up from Texas, but, few travelers stayed. Union Pacific's run for the coast crosses big Wyoming and has brought many a settler and settlement.

In this country where bigness is humbled, even the mighty Union Pacific is "put into its place" as shown on these two pages. At upper left, a Big Boy steams majestically west, up on high ground, over Sherman Hill in the late summer of 1956. At left, three big E-8s accelerate the eastbound *City of Portland* through the rugged country east of Green River. Above, looking for all the world like a doomsday creature, mammoth Big Boy spews forth its firey breath against the sun's open hearth, setting out to conquer Sherman Hill one more time. (WIDELL, DONAHUE, WIDELL)

"The difficult we do immediately, the impossible takes a little longer." The Denver and Rio Grande Western—often called "the Rebel of the Rockies"—*thrives* upon the mountains, with most of its beautifully maintained main line climbing and descending the Rockies between Denver and Pueblo to Salt Lake City and Ogden. Primarily a bridge-traffic carrying mountain climber, the railroad was possessed with massively handsome steam locomotives, well-suited for their daily Rocky Mountain tasks. At far left, of course, is the beautiful *California Zephyr* on its westward climb toward Moffat Tunnel and the highest main line crossing of any track in the U.S., Tennessee Pass, 10,240 feet above sea level. The power on this June 11, 1953, run is Alco PAs. At immediate left, one of the road's classically beautiful early series 4-8-4s gets a westbound military extra out of Bond, Colo., on a sparkling Oct. 9, 1950, amid the last trace of fall's golden aspen. Below, it's all black, grime, hard-business-as-usual for Rio Grande's giant 2-8-8-2 #3609 shoving hard on a coal train out of Minturn, Colo., on cold, cold May 11, 1953. What warm sun there is will soon be blotted out by the black breath of the L-131. At lower left, M-68 class Northern #1802 has a fast roll on the westbound *Royal Gorge,* out of Colorado Springs on Nov. 11, 1946. This handsome locomotive was built in 1938, along with four others, to supplement the road's 1700-series Northerns built ten years earlier. (VAN DUSEN, KERRIGAN, COLLECTION, COLLINS)

At upper left, on a magnificent autumn afternoon, Rio Grande's northbound freight heads up the narrow rails past "Jukes Tree," a mile out of Chama, N.M. In a few miles, the train will be in Colorado, on the way to the almost unbelievable climb up and over 10,015-ft.-high Cumbres Pass. At upper right is Rock Island's E-6 booster/box cab #750 in an almost "PR-type portrait," nearing Colorado Springs with the Colorado Springs' section of the *Rocky Mountain Rocket* on Dec. 7, 1946. This engine is one of the oddest diesels in America, and yet, from the standpoint of operations, one of the most practical. (More on this "quick change artist" in the text.) At right, the stunning, shining E-5s "Silver Racer" and "Silver Steed" make an elegant departure out of Colorado Springs in June, 1952, with the northbound *Texas Zephyr*. This beautiful train was inaugurated in August 1940, for service between Denver and Ft. Worth–Dallas over Burlington's subsidiaries Colorado & Southern and Ft. Worth & Denver. At lower left, two of Santa Fe's giant 2900-class 4-8-4s drift into a yellow block with the eastbound *Grand Canyon Limited's* northern section in June of 1950, near Wagon Mound, N.M., headed for La Junta, Colo., and ultimately Chicago. On board are several hundred Shriners returning from a convention in Los Angeles, and this section of No. 23 is one of over forty passenger trains running east today! Chances are both of the big Northerns will move the heavy train to Kansas City, where fresh power will be put on. (DONAHUE, HARLEY, KERRIGAN, WALLIN)

Certainly not one of Frisco's highly touted redballs, but nevertheless of great importance to the shippers it serves, is local freight No. 736 from Hugo, Okla., to Hope, Arkansas. GP-7 #617 has the head end honors today on the eastbound run, pictured going through the cattle guards at Idabel, Okla. The timetable advertises the fact that No. 736 "carries passengers in caboose," though "corpses will not be handled." At left, Cotton Belt's first passenger diesel, PA #300 waits for the highball out of Omaha, Texas—its St. Louis destination 601 miles away. Only two of the big Alcos were delivered (on Nov. 26, 1947) to the Cotton Belt (does *anyone* call it St. Louis Southwestern?). They were assigned the unlikely "steam locomotive sounding" classification Z-20s. PAs 300 and 301 are widely considered to have the most dashing—certainly the prettiest—paint schemes of any diesels in America.

On this page, and more my meat, May 15, 1945, finds a beautiful Rock Island R-67 class Northern heaving her heavy oily breath into the skies, backing to her train at Dalhart, Texas, a busy division point in the panhandle on the Kansas City–Tucumcari main. The Rock Island owned twenty of these big 5100-series 4-8-4s, ten of them coal burners, ten oil, for use on the east and west ends of the railroad. Below, and on another beautiful Texas day, in June 1955, Cotton Belt's Alco RS-3 #358 has the eastbound local freight in her grip, heading through Ridgeway, en route to Mt. Pleasant, approximately fifty miles away. (PLUMMER, PLUMMER, COLLINS, PLUMMER)

189

The trains of Texas! Of course we've all heard the story of the sales manager in Chicago who called his salesman in El Paso to quickly service a troublesome account in Texarkana, Texas. The Texas salesman was quick to respond, "Send someone to Texarkana from Chicago, it's closer!" He was right. And this gem helps underscore the fact that the huge state has more miles of railroad routes in it than any other state. All across Texas is the great Texas and Pacific Railway, and it is appropriate that I mention a booklet published in 1946 by T&P, celebrating their Diamond Jubilee: seventy-five years of service. *From Oxteams to Eagles* featured a profile of T&P's great 2-10-4 Texas type #600, the absolute embodiment of the strength of the railroad. Next to the photograph was the storyline: "The Southwest is on the threshold of a new era of industrial development, and, as it was nearly a century ago, the Texas and Pacific is in the vanguard of the parade of progress." Now, every book is entitled to at least one spoof! At left, giant Texas & Pacific 2-10-4 #610, in Texas, recreates the "parade of progress." At right, Cotton Belt's only FP-7, the dazzling #306, moves train No. 101 out of Mt. Pleasant, Texas. Below, two Texas and Pacific F-7s roll the high cars out of Mineola, Texas. Both diesel shots were taken in 1955; the 2-10-4 . . . (BALL, PLUMMER, PLUMMER)

191

The Southern Pacific . . . the railroad you can board and ride 3,184 miles in the same general direction without ever leaving the property! More specifically from New Orleans to L.A. to San Francisco, and on to Portland (using S.P.'s ferry to Oakland). 3,184 miles! The big and colorful railroad is well represented on this spread, from its beautiful motive power, to its long-distance freight and passenger runs, and its not-so-long commuter run. Above, it is Christmas 1955, and the diesels have changed things a little, having bumped the railroad's celebrated GS-4 Northerns off the *Daylight*. The E-7s and E-8 growl triumphantly through Chatsworth, having just come off the Santa Susanna Pass, heading the southbound *Daylight* toward Los Angeles. At right, and really in "no man's land," Espee's unique AC-9 cab-forward #4191 works a hotshot down the Alturos line through the high California desert near Termo on a beautiful evening, June 27, 1955. At lower right, the queen of Southern Pacific locomotives—the *Daylight* 4-8-4 (this sample being the 4458) heads into her stall at Taylor roundhouse Los Angeles, at the end of a glorious day, Dec. 22, 1954. She's just brought the *Daylight* down from San Francisco—O.T. At immediate right, almost out-of-place 80"-drivered MT-4 Mountain #4337 takes a commute out of San Francisco on a penninsula run in August 1956. For those of us who missed main line Southern Pacific steam, the forty-seven-mile commuter line offered one more final chance to see big Espee passenger steam at work. (KERRIGAN, BALL, PICKETT, WIDELL)

James J. Hill's classic statement upon his retirement from the Great Northern Railway has been quoted many, many times yet bears repeating: "Most men who have really lived have had, in some shape, their great adventure. This railway is mine." Some of the "great adventure" went into the building of all three of the northern transcontinentals, and perhaps the scene, at right, of Great Northern's magnificent *Empire Builder* passing along the southern boundary of Glacier Park in Montana's rugged Rockies, best portrays the task that first faced Jim Hill. Below, two pairs of Z-1 class motors head into the Wenatchee, Wash., yard after bringing a 2,900-ton train "over the hill"—a maximum 2.2 percent grade—on the Cascade line from Skykomish, Wash., on June 22, 1955. At lower left, the brakeman rides his engine, one of Milwaukee's classic EP-2 bipolar electrics, running around the *Olympian* in Seattle to pull the train backward over to Tacoma in October 1949. At immediate left, a beautiful, almost delicate study of Northern Pacific steam power at Livingston, Mont. on Jan. 20, 1946. (HARLEY, BOGEN, WALLIN COLLECTION, PICKETT)

196

"There is no easy way to get there!" I'm sure the builders of all seven transcontinentals said this many times, pondering over ways of crossing the Continental Divide to reach the West Coast. For the three big railroads coming into southern California—the Southern Pacific, Union Pacific and Santa Fe—there was the additional hurdle of crossing the rugged mountains of the Coast Range. In the 1870s, Santa Fe's track was laid down across the flat Mojave Desert, but then the builders came smack up against the formidable San Bernardino Mountains. From Victorville to the summit of Cajon Pass, the rails were spiked down (I should say up!) upon nineteen miles of 1.5 percent grade, with an even steeper 3 percent descent down the western slope. Cajon Pass was opened in 1885, and since then, the arrival of a transcontinental train from the east has symbolized man's great accomplishment of crossing the western frontier.

The arrival of Santa Fe transcontinentals into Los Angeles fittingly close this look at America's colorful railroads. Below, the last rays of the setting sun glint off the squared flanks of Santa Fe's A-B-B-A Alco PAs heading through the curve below the summit of Cajon, passing Union Pacific's eastbound *City of Los Angeles* which will run over the tracks of the Santa Fe as far as Daggett, nine miles east of Barstow. At far left, the first glimpse of train No. 23, the *Grand Canyon Limited* rounding the bend that leads into Los Angeles Union Passenger Terminal (LAUPT). At lower left, the *Grand Canyon Limited* is shown again, making its entrance into LA past Mission tower, its Alco power smoking things up, as usual. At immediate left, the PA's handsome face is shown at bumper post's end at LAUPT. (CAJON-WALLIN COLLECTION; *all others,* BALL)

¡Viva Vapor, y tú tambien Baldwin cienpies!
And live on they did, in Mexico, affording
many of us in the trackside audience one last
encore of big steam, early diesels, and of
course, 3-foot narrow gauge. After 1960, when
U.S. and Canadian main line steam was gone,
we turned to Mexico—really out of
desperation—only to be beautifully surprised
by the fact that Mexican railroading took us
back a couple of decades into better times.
Many of us did not know the ghost of the 1938
20th-Century Limited was still in Mexico in
the form of ex-New York Central passenger
cars from that train, or that early-to-dieselize
Florida East Coast was alive in Flagler's
4-8-2s. Many of us forgot that Nickel Plate,
Norfolk Southern and Chicago & North Western steam had migrated south to Mexico. And

it's interesting to note we're talking about
steam that had vanished early from U.S. rails
but became available at a perfect time to meet
the needs of Mexico. Ironically, when the cur-
tain finally fell on our finest in steam, it was
too late for their salvation in dieselizing
Mexico. Discovering the steam locomotives
that we never really got to know in the U.S.
was a pure delight!

In the 1960s, the National Railroad of
Mexico dispatched an onslaught of steam-
powered trains each morning out of Valle de
Mexico, north of Mexico City. From before
dawn, 'til siesta, everything left town for their
day's work, and the pursuing rail-
photographer was confronted with many rail
lines that all seemingly went nowhere, in opposite directions, where there were no roads!

The formidable looking HR-4 class 2-6-6-2,
above, heads northward out of Valle, bound for
Tolteca under an unusually beautiful silvery
sky. The 2033 was built by American Locomotive in 1938 and was Mexico's largest-in-
steam. The largest-in-diesels is well represented by N de M's huge Baldwin centipede,
at upper right, ready to depart Saltillo with no
less than 3,000 h.p. and twenty-four wheels!
At lower right, and I think the most stunning
picture in this book, two oil-burning narrow
gauge class G-030 consolidations roll freight
down to Puebla over the stone viaduct near
Ozumba. The 17,880-ft.-high Popocatepetl
Volcano looms in the distance. Besides freight,
there is daily passenger service over this
3-ft.-gauge line between Mexico City and Peu-
bla. (DONAHUE, WALLIN COLLECTION, DONAHUE)

Burlington's E-5 diesel #9912A heads the westbound *Morning Zephyr* toward a station stop at Oregon, Ill., in December 1964. Tolerable caption? Diesel? Obviously I've styled this caption for the period in which the picture was taken. But look again. This is a fluted, stainless steel, slant-nosed EMD from pre-war days, when *Zephyr* was fashionable. And undoubtedly this engine dazzled many a youth, just the way Rock Island's *Rocket* did me, and the way so many pioneer diesel streamliners flashing across the pages of Lucius Beebe's book's did. But look again; it's the 1960s and we've come full cycle with diesels. Never mind the fact that 9912A is a *survivor* in her own right . . . Never mind the fact she once proudly wore her own shining nameplate "Silver Meteor," and even wore silver skirts covering her less than

shiny wheels. She, well diesels, had pushed steam off the rails everywhere—and that's what mattered. 9912A was to be resented. In three years she'd be unceremoniously traded in to EMD, right back from where she came, for a more powerful SD-40 freight diesel. It did not matter . . . one diesel would simply replace another. But look again—here is authentic glamour, beauty and escape from the angular, boxy diesels we always see. Here is a profile of a full-bosomed woman that commands enough respect and attention to be immortalized in a pan shot by a railfan.

Stay around, old "Silver Meteor"; I'd like more people to see what Diesel really was. Or is! Will you be back this way tomorrow? (BOYD)

EPILOGUE

AN INTENSE SPOT OF GREEN burned from the CTC signal to the west as train time neared at Oregon, Ill. This was the Chicago to Minneapolis main line of the CB&Q, and I was waiting for Train 21, the westbound *Morning Zephyr* on a sunny December morning in 1964. According to Donald Steffee's authoritative speed survey in *Trains* Magazine, No. 21's scheduled coverage of the 45.2 miles across the Illinois cornfields between Aurora and Rochelle in 33 minutes for an *average* speed of 82.3 mph made it the fastest scheduled train in the country. I knew from past experience that the *Zephyr* met that demanding schedule with well over 90 mph running wherever the track was straight enough for the engineer to turn 'em loose.

We were very proud of the *Zephyr* in our part of the country, but on this particular morning, speed statistics were incidental to the anticipation of what might be on the point of today's No. 21. The railfan grapevine had spread the word that two of the Burlington's original 1940 E5 passenger diesels had been assigned to the *Zephyr* pool and had been showing up regularly on No. 21.

With elegantly slanted noses, the E5's were the last survivors of the pre-war era of custom-built diesel locomotives. Sheathed in gleaming fluted stainless steel to match the Budd-built passenger cars, the Burlington's E5's were the only engines of their style ever built. The economic pressures of mass production during and after World War II precluded such custom touches on virtually all the diesels that followed—some Burlington, Père Marquette and *Texas Special* E7s after the war got some stainless paneling, but not the full treatment like the E5s.

The sound of a chime horn drifted in from the east, and a moment later a silver nose popped into the trusswork of the bridge over the Rock River. That's it! An E5. Check the camera . . . film advanced . . . shutter speed set at 1/30th of a second . . . exposure correct . . . here it comes . . . lock the viewfinder onto the cab window and follow the motion . . . pan across and *snap!* Oh boy, this should be a great shot if it works, but a pan shot is always tricky and as much luck as skill.

The engine was 9912A, and its stainless steel was as brilliant as it had been when the La Grange factory put it on in March 1940. The rigors of time and maintenance forces had cost the unit its skirting over the trucks—I never cared for that touch anyhow—and the name "Silver Meteor" on its side panels, but that twenty-four-year veteran was still in good enough condition to be entrusted with the fastest train in the country. The picture I got back a week later showed it all: the engine, the sunshine, the speed.

That picture sums up a lot of the rewards of being a railfan photographer. As a satisfying leisure time activity, railfanning is probably more of a sport than a hobby, and it shares much of the same incentives as hunting. The railfan carries a camera instead of a gun, but he stalks his prey in much the same manner as the hunter. The railfan decides what he wants to "capture," learns its whereabouts and habits, and pits his skill and knowledge against the elusiveness of the beast and the trickery of the environment and weather. Like the hunter who must combine the technical knowledge and skill of firearms with the sensitivity of the ways of nature, the railfan must master the workings of his cameras in addition to learning the ways of the railroads.

Railfanning today is a growing and energetic hobby with four general circulation national magazines—in addition to three magazines devoted principally to model railroading—and an entire network of specialty publications ranging from slick and professional efforts devoted to such topics as passenger trains and locomotive technology to historical and technical newsletters of local organizations and groups devoted to the study of one particular railroad or region.

The seasoned railfan can now venture into almost any area of the country already armed with references gleaned from various publications that can tell him each railroad's entire roster of locomotives, the details of its day-to-day operations, a list of the radio frequencies used by the company radios—to go with the relatively inexpensive radio scanners that permit the railfans to listen directly to train/dispatcher/depot communications—and usually local reports only hours old as to what is running where. The weather can still dampen the day, but with top quality, high speed color film and state-of-the-art cameras with through-the-lens light meters, even the most severe weather conditions can't stop a well equipped and determined railfan.

This was not always the case. In the 1940s and 1950s, when most of the photos in this book were taken, the railfan community was composed of tiny groups of widely scattered "lone wolves" or a few friends who shared an interest in train pictures. The two national railfan publications at that time, *Railroad* and *Trains* magazines, used almost no color, and the entire focus of rail photography concentrated on large-format black-and-white work. The photographers had to learn their craft individually, for the most part, with only the material printed in the magazines and a few pictorial railroad books for reference and a means of judging their own work.

In the years after World War II there were fine cameras and films available for black-and-white work, but the film sizes and incredibly slow emulsion speeds of the color films virtually precluded their use with the same techniques that were normal for black and white. Really good 35mm cameras that were ideal for color slide work (the rangefinder Leica was generally considered the best in its day) were rather expensive, and most of the old-line steam photographers felt much more comfortable with their big cameras and black-and-white glossy prints that could be collected, shared and published. Color was fun, but there was little market for it beyond a rare magazine cover and simple entertainment.

For the most part, the color photographers of the 1940s and 1950s were not the same people whose names were becoming recognizable in the photo credits of publications. The color photographers were a largely obscure lot until relatively recent years when the expanding railfan publications began developing a market for color photography. Through the increased use of color in railfan magazines and books, the true pioneers of color rail photography are finally finding a place to share their efforts and experiences with the hobby in general.

The problems these early color photographers faced are hard to imagine in this day of excellent ASA 64 and 200 color transparency films and superb 35mm cameras. In the 1940s, the best of the color slide films was Kodachrome—the *original* Kodachrome of ASA 10! What that film speed meant to the rail photographer was that a bright sunlit exposure was 1/200th of a second at f3.5, if you were fortunate enough to have a lens that would open up to f3.5. In layman's terms, the slow film speed meant that if you got the shutter speed up to where you could do a reasonable job of "stopping" a moving train, you had the lens "wide open" at its least desirable setting; to get a better lens setting you had to sacrifice shutter speed to the point where a moving train would simply blur. With photographers working at the ragged edge of the camera's abilities, it's not surprising that much of the early color photography lacks the creative touch that we take for granted today.

In their quest for a faster color film, many photographers turned to wierd brands of domestic and imported film. Under ideal conditions Kodak's Kodachrome was the best, but it was much too slow for most action work. Kodak's Ektachrome was faster, but it was less sharp and its color rendition tended to be imprecise. Those who got good results with the early Ektachrome and other films were often disappointed later when the lack of "permanence" in the chemistry would cause the slides to lose or shift color after years of storage. An unfortunate number of priceless photos that were perfect right after they were shot are useless today because the film wouldn't age.

Some of the earlier 35mm cameras were pretty awful, too. To those of us who grew up with any of the modern single lens reflexes (SLRs), when somebody says "it's got a bad lens," you can be pretty sure he's just a lousy photographer who's making excuses for his own ineptitude. But back in the '40s and early '50s, the early 35mm cameras often did have lenses that simply weren't sharp.

And if the lens happened to be good, sometimes the shutter wasn't. One of the most popular modestly-priced 35mm cameras of the time was the Argus C-3, the beloved old "brick." It had a nasty habit of "vignetting" the corners of the picture with the action of its rather slow blade shutter—any photos you see with the corners of the sky darkened you can bet were shot with a C-3. They had good lenses and decent shutter speeds, but with the C-3 you just had to live with dark skies.

The years between the end of World War II and 1960 were exciting yet frustrating for railfans from the standpoints of both photography and the railroad scene itself. The diesel was here to stay, but steam was still making its grand final showing. Steam fans were concentrating on the last stands of their locomotives with a sense of urgency that only the news of impending dieselization could generate. Although the diesels were clean and colorful, they were resented for the way they decimated the ranks of the steam engines. Most of the steam photographers refused to take pictures of the shiny intruders. To be a diesel fan was heresy.

To those of us who were just coming of age during this period, the transition from steam to diesel was a rending experience of affection and sudden, bitter loss. Just when we began to truly understand and appreciate the steam locomotive, it was suddenly torn away and replaced by the dreaded diesel. I didn't know what a large part trains and cameras would play in my life when I moved with my parents in 1949 to a house that looked out across the railroad tracks, but my experiences in becoming a railfan and learning photography are probably typical of many hobbyists of the era.

Those beautiful deep steamboat whistles of the Illinois Central Mikados were a part of my grade school years from 1949 to early 1955. My home in Dixon, Ill., was only a block for the Squires Avenue crossing, the first of six that a northbound freight would encounter as it hammered up through the north side of town. The Amboy District of the Springfield Division was known locally as "the Gruber," an odd name whose origin is lost somewhere in history. The Gruber was the home of husky 2-8-2s, mostly 2100s with a handful of 1200–1500s to keep things interesting.

The resident switch engine was a good-sized 0-6-0 that could easily pass for one of the road engines in the character of its exhause and whistle tone. The 341 was our regular switcher, and she would alternate with 313, 259 and 275 in the early 1950s as she would take her monthly trek to Freeport for inspections. You could almost set your watch by the switch crew's afternoon run up to "the Colony" (the local state hospital) to deliver coal to its power plant.

Even a twelve-year-old could learn wheel arrangements and train numbers if he had a railfan friend of the worldly age of fourteen. I was fortunate to have met Chet French one afternoon while watching the 0-6-0 switch the Borden plant behind my grandparents' house down on the highway. Two years is quite an age barrier when you're in grade school, but finding someone else who knew the difference between a Mikado and a Mountain was enough to bridge the gap, and we became close friends. Chet was the first "railfan" I ever met aside from myself, and we shared experiences and learned from each other more of that great world of railroading than we would ever have explored had each of us remained alone. At this age, however, a camera was an expensive and forbidden object stashed away in the parents' dresser drawer.

The Gruber put on its show for us with Mikados on the "noon locals" and the evening southbound freight No. 373. The 0-6-0 was always somewhere around, but the sport would be to spot unusual engines or equipment from the dining room window or from the back yard whenever one of those booming whistles would interrupt work on the basement model railroad or a two-man softball game up in the field. Light Pacific 1002 rolling north dead-in-tow was the highlight of one entire summer, but the sight of a live 2-10-2, 2810, the next year on a southbound Dunbar ore train was the most impressive locomotive I'd ever seen.

A birthday present Kodak Brownie box camera managed to capture some blurred images of Mikados at Squires Avenue, but those grade school years were otherwise devoted to nothing more permanent than rapt observation and a few jotted engine numbers.

And suddenly it was gone.

Black diesels replaced the Mikados and the 0-6-0 almost overnight in the late winter of early 1955. Chime air horns were no replacement for steamboat whistles, and nothing, absolutely nothing, could replace the sound of a 2-8-2 on a northbounder charging for the grade.

My bicycle became my means to get all the way across town to see the big Pacifics that still pulled the "Clinton passenger" through town on the Chicago & North Western. The depot on the south side of town was as alien as a foreign country to a northsider like myself. But growing up means expanding one's horizons, and in a couple of months I would be going to high school. It was only right that I should learn to accept the C&NW as my "other" railroad.

But suddenly the Pacifics were gone, too.

By the end of the summer of 1955 there were only diesels running through Dixon. Then began the parade of dead steam locomotives. Southbound, southbound, always southbound, the rusting hulks began showing up in the trains passing through on the IC. In later years I would learn that they were bound for cutting torches at Paducah and Granite City, but then I only knew they were southbound.

Dead engines were parading through Dixon in vastly greater variety than had ever shown up live. Lumbering 0-8-0s and elegant 2400-Class 4-8-2s that I had known only as pictures in Bill Whitbeck's article in the treasured March 1953 issue of *Trains & Travel* were suddenly showing up back in the consists of southbound freights. Here I was finally seeing engines I had yearned to see for years, but they were all dead!

It was a bittersweet experience, but youth is not a time of life that lends itself to sentimental mourning. Chet was already beginning to "groove" on the pure sound of the black GP7s and GP9s that had displaced our steam engines. Sure enough, you could hear them revving up as they came across the bridge, and just before reaching Squires Avenue they would suddenly idle back, make "transition" and load up again with a soul-satisfying surge. Recognizing that sound was my first reluctant step toward "making my peace" with the diesel.

In the spring of 1956 Chet and I got our last look at IC steam in regular service as we spent a week visiting his grandparents in Forrest and his Aunt Nelda in Chatsworth. The "Bloomer" ran through Chatsworth, that being the IC's Bloomington to Kankakee branch that we knew was populated by 900-Class 2-8-0s. We had a bet going as to what engine would be on the job the day we saw it; Chet said the 908 and I felt sure it would be the 906. My triumph was unbounded as 906 banged across the TP&W diamond and pulled up next to the grain elevator. It switched a couple of cars as I frantically rapped off snapshots with my new Brownie Hawkeye. With a fine display of smoke and steam it left town, and Chet and I both stood in a tense and tingling silence to listen to its last sounds as it topped the hill. The agony was prolonged as it stopped just at the edge of our sight and hearing to make a setout at Diller's tile plant north of town. And then it, too, was gone.

We knew that was probably the last IC steam either of us would ever see, but our feeling was one of gratitude for the privilege of one last look rather than a depressing sense of loss. A pair of green and tan RS2s on the TP&W made for a quick diversion, and the next day spent on the Wabash at Forrest with brilliant blue, white and gray diesels was a show teenage railfans couldn't resist. Chet's uncle drove the mail truck that met the overnight passenger train, and he "arranged" for the two of us to ride the cab of the GP7 on Wabash No. 18, *The Midnight,* as far as Orland Park on our way home. Steam was gone and diesels were here to stay, so why fight it?

True to the pattern, horizons were widening. The Northwestern Steel & Wire mill in nearby Sterling, Ill., was still being switched by ex-CB&Q 0-6-0s, and their scrap line was a veritable museum of big steam locomotives pausing on their way to oblivion. There were actually New York Central Hudsons and Burlington 2-10-2s and C&NW Class H 4-8-4s there rusting away their final moments before meeting the scrapper's torch. Every time Chet or I could beg or borrow the family car it was over to Sterling to see what new had shown up. After a trek through the condemned hulks, we would go down to Miller Street or the Avenue G crossing and watch the live 0-6-0s slamming cars about, recreating a caricature image of our IC memories.

It was in 1957 that I discovered the "fan trip." The Railroad Club of Chicago was running an excursion around the Chicago terminal district on the Baltimore & Ohio Chicago Terminal Company using a B&O Mikado. My paper route was a source of modest income, so I saved enough for a ticket into Chicago on the C&NW and the fan trip on the B&OCT. It was wonderful; there I was riding behind a steam engine on a railroad I'd never seen before except in the pages of magazines.

The ticket purchase for the B&O trip got me on the mailing list for future fan trips, and the CB&Q was just warming up to the business. Suddenly steam engines were available again to me at predictable places and times. Burlington 4-8-4s and 2-8-2s. DM&IR 2-8-8-4s. Grand Trunk 4-8-4s. All I had to do was save my money and buy a ticket.

I knew there were still 2-8-4s running somewhere on the Nickel Plate and that the N&W was still running 2-8-8-2s in the mountains, but these were strange and distant places, and Chet wouldn't trust his car over about 50 miles. "Real" steam seemed always just beyond my reach. By the time I could get to Fort Wayne, the Nickel Plate 2-8-4s were in Bellevue. By the time I could get to Bellevue the Berks were gone and I'd have to go to the N&W. I could never seem to meet somebody who knew how to seek out the remaining steam operations, so I simply kept scampering off after the fan trips. It was unfortunate for me, because I know now that there was much within relatively easy reach if I'd only had someone to show the way. Kentucky, West Virginia and Canada, where steam was still running, might as well have been on the moon.

By now I was entrusted with my dad's Zeiss-Ikon camera (even though I didn't really understand how to use it) and my own second-hand 8mm movie camera bought with money earned at my first "real" job, running a blueprint machine for a local civil engineer who also happened to be a model railroader. A graduation present fan trip behind Burlington 4-8-4s to Colorado for three days on the Rio Grande narrow gauge marked my departure from high school in the spring of 1959. On our "free day" in Denver, I managed to link up with four others who rented a car to drive up to Cheyenne for a look at the Union Pacific and Colorado & Southern. Everything was dead on the UP, but there were Challengers and 4-8-4s stored outside and fourteen Big Boys in the roundhouse that were cold but otherwise ready to go. At least I had caught a glimpse of the biggest before they were all gone.

The C&S showed some life, though, and just as we were about to leave they chuffed 2-8-2 803 onto the turntable and out onto the ready track for the evening local. That was the last look I would ever get at regular service main line steam.

That autumn I entered the University of Illinois at Champaign, and through a friendly tower operator made the acquaintence of some of the resident railfans. "J. Parker Lamb, Jr." was a name I'd seen under many photographs in *Trains* Magazine, and that awesome upperclassman showed a remarkable hospitality toward an eager but bumbling freshman who happened to be a railfan. Having just returned from photographing the last season of steam operation on the IC main line, Parker Lamb was the traveling railfan who could finally teach me how to take good pictures and seek out steam. But that steam was now gone, at least from the world I felt I could reach.

It was sometime during that first semester at Champaign that I met another railfan who was visiting the campus. Don Ball was a few years older than myself, and he was chasing back and forth across the country grasping the last fragments of steam operation. He had mastered the workings of a camera and learned the ways of the railroads at an early age, and thanks to a Kansas driver's license he got at age 14, his was the world of B&O EM1s out of Benwood, CNJ camelbacks and IC 2800s on coal drags. He was clinging tenaciously to the fragmenting world of steam railfanning that by circumstance of birth and geography I had just missed.

Don was one of the last and youngest of the true steam-era railfans. He had grown up with UP 4-12-2s, Rock Island 4-8-4s and Santa Fe Hudsons in Kansas and learned photography in time to capture them on film. He pursued the retreating armies of steam engines and over the next several years came to know first-hand the shower of cinders from Reading 4-8-4s in the anthracite country, the grace of the L&N's 2-8-4s out of DeCoursey and the ear-splitting shriek of Pennsy K4s at speed in the night. He had lived the railroading I had known only through the pages of *Trains* Magazine.

The only steam experiences Don and I were to share would be on fan trips. On October 24, 1959, the L&N borrowed IC 4-8-2 2613 for an anniversary fan trip between Louisville and Nashville—the L&N had no steamers of its own left. The trip gave me my first look at a live IC Mountain. Don was there too, but he was using the trip as an opportunity to relive previous experiences with similar engines. He concentrated on the locomotive and tried to ignore the circumstances of the trip itself, finding an L&N passenger consist full of railfans alien to his memories of 2600s on the IC.

We spent most of the trip in the baggage car right behind the engine where we could lean out on the special railings across the door openings to see and hear the locomotive work. Someone discovered that the front door of the baggage car had not been locked and we could open it up and look right at the back of the tender. As we were ascending one of the more difficult grades on the line, Don was taken by the idea of reliving a ride he'd had on the tender of a 2600 on the IC main line a few years before.

When he got the opportunity, he went through the front door of the baggage car and onto the walkway on the back of 2613's tender, quickly scampering up the back ladder and onto the deck of the tank. He wrapped his arms around the safety railings and hung on for the ride. It must have been superb up there until we encountered something that you don't find on the IC main line: a tunnel.

We hit that tunnel working wide open and Don was suddenly overwhelmed in smoke and steam. He nearly passed out and needed help to get down from the lofty perch. I don't remember the exact words, but two sentences seemed to come out together, "What happened?" and "Boy, was that great!"

In his world of steam, fan trips were an intrusion into Don Ball's reality. For me, fan trips were the only steam reality I would know. Parker Lamb, on the other hand, was far more interested in *railroading* than in any particular type of motive power. Oh, he was out on the IC when 4-8-2s were running, but when steam became inconveniently remote, he was just as happy to photograph the ever-present diesels. Because he was not strictly a steam fan, he had acquired a reputation as a "diesel photographer." That was an oversimplification of how Parker Lamb looked at things because he had turned his camera toward the drama of contemporary railroading and was showing trains working in their natural surroundings. Whether the engine was steam or diesel didn't seem to matter much to him.

I couldn't have had a better teacher. Parker introduced me to good cameras and taught me how to use them. He even sold me one of his trusted Kodak Chevron 2¼"-square rangefinder cameras. "This is the only camera in the country that you can run a roll of film through and don't even have to open the shutter to get trains on the negative," he joked. (It was that same camera I used for the E5 pan shot.)

Parker took me, with my new Chevron in hand, lineside, and we photographed IC streamliners ripping through Tuscola at 100 mph and got pan shots from his car riding alongside an IC E6. We went to Forrest and shot Wabash Train Masters and TP&W F3s in the snow. This was the style of photography that he was making famous in *Trains,* and although I didn't fully appreciate it at the time, I was being exposed to the type of railfan photography that would typify the next decade. Parker Lamb was primarily a black-and-white photographer shooting for magazine publication. I don't recall him shooting any color, and the idea of color photography never entered my mind except for the 8mm movies. This was quite a contrast to today's railfanning when almost everybody starts out shooting color of some kind.

When I left the UofI for photography school a year or so later, I rather quickly left the ways of Parker Lamb and his diesels and reverted back to my own passion for steam—in this case, primarily fan trip steam. As part of my schooling, I began to shoot color transparencies, but always as the second camera along with the black and white for railfan subjects.

I can almost pin down the moment when I started shooting diesels in color simply because they were interesting and fun. In June 1963 Bruce Bailey and I were well into our second day of photographing the Duluth & Northeastern, a steam operated short line in Minnesota, when we knocked off early in the afternoon and headed for Duluth to shoot the diesels of the DM&IR, DSS&A, GN, NP and Soo Line. That was the turning point for me, and I suddenly found diesels to be colorful and fascinating subjects for the camera.

One could make a good case that photographing diesels in black and white was worthwhile, but shooting diesels in color was a lot more fun. If railfanning was going to be a hobby, then color slides were the way to go. I still couldn't shake my old black and white habits, though, and I began shooting both black and white and color slides of almost everything. I was developing hopes of getting some of my pictures published, and the magazines still demanded mostly black and white.

Magazines. There's that word again. What an important part they played in my life as a railfan and what an impact they must have on others. Books are beauty and documentation and permanence, but magazines are news and now and information to be used. I had learned of the railroads beyond my home town through the pages of *Trains* and *Railroad,* and the photography I practiced reflected their needs and ideas.

The magazines made it possible for the hobby to communicate with itself. Editors influenced how the hobby developed by the material they selected for print. *Railroad* Magazine had a proud and long history dating back into the 1920s when railroaders were interested in trains, and the hobby and industry were comprised of generally the same people. Railroaders were woven into the fabric of American life, and a magazine like *Railroad* could prosper on history, true stories, fiction and advertisements for Calvert Blended Whiskies and International Correspondence Schools.

Railfans and modelers were granted token column space in the pulp pages of the old *Railroad,* but for the most part it devoted itself to the working railroaders. Its "Engine Picture Club" promoted the fine art of exacting roster photography, and action photography was pretty much limited to publicity glossies and the railfan's traditional "smoking wedge" coming-on views. The steam locomotive was such an inherently photogenic beast that little creativity was required—the "arty" photography that did show up was likely to be of the camera club salon contest type.

In 1940, Al Kalmbach in Milwaukee started up a small but slick paper monthly called *Trains* Magazine, a publication for the rail hobbyist and not the working railroader. Almost immediately it set the lead in photography style and content. *Trains* editors encouraged the more imaginative and journalistic photographers and demanded more of a photo than a rods-down three-quarter view with the smoke laying back. Night photography and creative interpretations of all aspects of the railroad scene were given space in print.

It was a good thing, too, because by the early 1950s when it became clear to all who would look that the steam engine was doomed, the caliber of railfan photography had been elevated to a level that permitted steam's last few years to be documented with a quality and sensitivity that simply wouldn't have been possible a decade earlier.

And the Age of the Diesel would require much more of the photographer than steam ever had. The steam engine displayed its entire workings for the world to see with smoke and steam to animate its every mood. The diesel wrapped its secrets under its hood and left a barely visible trace at the stack and trackside to give evidence to its actions. In simple terms, a diesel doing 60 looked just like a diesel standing still.

In the years following the end of steam in 1960, the railfan community developed an entirely new set of skills and values. Instead of dying off with the end of steam, the hobby grew at a staggering rate in an effort to record and preserve every moment of the rapidly changing railroad scene. The railfans formed new organizations, breathed new life into old ones and began communicating with each other through magazines, books, newsletters and meetings. One segment realized that the earliest history of the diesel was only crudely documented and set about researching the technical development back to the diesel's Year One.

And some new heroes began to emerge. Out of the ranks of the old-line steam photographers filtered a few who admitted to the heresy of taking pictures of the early diesels. Often scorned in the 1940s and '50s by their diesel-hating peers, the photographers who shot the shiny intruders anyway were finding an intense interest in their work. Crusty old steam photographers were often baffled by the uproar that a picture of "some old diesel" caused when a sharp-eyed youngster would spot it as a rare variant of a pre-war Alco.

Times and values change, and as the content of this book demonstrates, both steam and diesel are now considered worthy subjects from the 1940s and '50s. The black-and-white photographers have kept us up with the times by documenting the decades and sharing their rail experiences with us over the years in all types of publications. At a time when railfan activity has never been greater, it's satisfying to see the hobby searching out its own roots and now having the opportunity to pay tribute to those who captured on color film the heritage of America's colorful railroads.

Newton, New Jersey   Jim Boyd
                                                      RAILFAN Magazine